THE GARDEN
PROBLEM SOLVER

Staff for Successful Gardening (U.S.A.)
Editor: Carolyn T. Chubet

Contributors
Editor: Thomas Christopher
Art Editor: Joan Gramatte
Editorial Assistant: Troy Dreier
Consulting Editor: Lizzie Boyd (U.K.)
Consultant: Dora Galitzki
Copy Editor: Sue Heinemann
Art Assistant: Antonio Mora

READER'S DIGEST GENERAL BOOKS
Editor in Chief: John A. Pope, Jr.
Managing Editor: Jane Polley
Executive Editor: Susan J. Wernert
Art Director: David Trooper
Group Editors: Will Bradbury, Sally French,
Norman B. Mack, Kaari Ward
Group Art Editors: Evelyn Bauer, Robert M. Grant, Joel Musler
Chief of Research: Laurel A. Gilbride
Copy Chief: Edward W. Atkinson
Picture Editor: Richard Pasqual
Head Librarian: Jo Manning

The credits and acknowledgments that appear on page 176
are hereby made a part of this copyright page.

Originally published in partwork form.
Copyright © 1990 Eaglemoss Publications Ltd.

Based on the edition copyright © 1993
The Reader's Digest Association Limited.

Library of Congress Cataloging in Publication Data

The Garden problem solver
    p.   cm. — (Successful gardening)
Includes index.
ISBN 0-89577-675-8
   1. Landscape gardening.   2. Landscape gardening—Pictorial works.
I. Reader's Digest Association. II. Series.
SB473.G2888   1994
635.9'5—dc20   94-30615

Printed in the United States of America

Opposite: On alkaline soil, a dense shelter belt of hydrangeas develop
bronze-red instead of blue flowers.

Overleaf: Evergreen pyracanthas can solve many problems, since they are
indifferent to soil type and situation.

THE READER'S DIGEST ASSOCIATION, INC.
Pleasantville, New York / Montreal

SUCCESSFUL GARDENING

THE GARDEN PROBLEM SOLVER

CONTENTS

Problem sites

Shady and damp sites

Gardening on acid soil

Gardening on alkaline soil

Problem site Grassy slopes cut up with garden beds turn mowing into a tiresome challenge.

Problem sites

No gardener would admit to having a perfect location, but some sites are more difficult to manage than others. Neglected and overgrown plots can, with dedicated work, be turned into attractive gardens, but unsightly features inside and outside a garden's borders are often very difficult to convert into a beautiful view.

Sloping gardens are hard to cultivate, as the soil usually drains too freely and is often in danger of being washed away. The most sensible solution is to terrace the problem site into a series of level beds with retaining walls. In this way, you can also create sheltered microclimates on the lower terraces for choice but cold-sensitive plants. Some slopes can be covered with grass, but others are too steep to make mowing anything but a backbreaking chore. In these situations, ground covers and mat-forming shrubs are easier to deal with and excellent for anchoring the soil.

Gardens by the sea or on windswept open sites may be protected by planting windbreaks — hedges or irregular belts of shrubs and trees. However, if you live near the sea, you will learn that a storm may carry salt spray many miles inland, so it is wisest to plant only those species that can tolerate such a dousing. Fortunately, there are many.

Should you decide to install a swimming pool in your garden, you will find that it immediately becomes the landscape's focal point. Treat it accordingly, and let the planting play a secondary but supporting role.

Long-term neglect Drastic pruning and deep rototilling will be the first steps toward restoring this garden.

GARDEN REHABILITATION

Bringing a neglected garden back to life requires ruthless removal of plants that are past their prime, weed eradication, and thorough soil improvement.

As you begin the challenging task of reclaiming a neglected garden, first plan the new garden you intend to make. Draw a rough sketch on a piece of paper, and make a list of the new materials and plants you will need. Anything that can be salvaged is a bonus, whether it is a few spring bulbs, a wall or path, or an overgrown but rescuable specimen tree.

Clearing the site

First, make a detailed survey of the garden to determine the scale of its problems and decide what can be saved and what must be removed.

Ideally, you should tackle the renovation gradually, spreading the work out over several seasons. Otherwise, you may unwittingly destroy seasonal flowers such as bulbs or wildflowers, which appear only at certain times of the year. Besides, pruning trees and shrubs is most successful when carried out in the proper seasons. Getting control of weeds is a gradual process, too. Begin by cutting and removing the brush and overgrowth, then dig up the roots. Some roots, however, will almost certainly escape and send up new shoots, which must also be destroyed.

Eradicate perennial weeds as soon as possible as they will be difficult to deal with later. Either dig them out, which is environmentally friendly but hard work, or apply appropriate herbicides.

Start clearing the weeds during early spring, when growth begins. Digging or rototilling should expose the weeds' roots; remove every bit of aggressive species such as bindweed and nettles, as they will quickly resprout from any small root fragments you overlook. If you dump the debris into the compost pile, make sure that these tough and long-lived roots don't survive to become a problem again when you spread the compost in your garden.

If your garden is large, divide it into manageable units, and tackle them one at a time. As each unit is cleared, it is important to eliminate annual weeds before they can set seed, removing them either by hand or with a hoe.

One of the most effective herbicides for both perennial and annual weeds is glyphosate, a nonselective contact weed killer. If the garden is overgrown with brush, you may have to resort to a brush killer such as triclopyr as well. Handle all such chemicals carefully, according to the manufacturer's directions.

For areas of limited size, a watering can fitted with a fine rose provides an easy means of application. Choose a windless, dry day for this task, to prevent

◀ **Signs of neglect** Overgrown hedges, straggly roses, and weed-infested gardens all cry out for attention. With the tangled undergrowth and perennial weeds out of the way, attend first to the fences, then plan a new design on paper before doing major pruning operations and relaying the paths and patio.

spray from drifting onto other plants or onto you. For large areas, use a compressor sprayer or one of the types that screws onto the end of a garden hose. Keeping the spray pressure low produces larger droplets of weed killer and reduces the drift onto nontarget areas. Wear rubber gloves and any other protective gear called for by the product label. When applying herbicides in a mixture with water, mix only as much solution as is needed for the task at hand. Do not pour leftover solution down a storm drain.

Apply chemical weed killers in spring, when plants are growing vigorously. Spray methodically in a series of overlapping sweeps. Divide large gardens into manageable sections, and if neces-

sary, spread the work over several days.

When systemic herbicides such as glyphosate or 2,4-D are used, plants may take several weeks to wilt and die. Some very hardy weeds may need two applications.

Some chemicals, such as glyphosate, are inactivated on contact with the soil, and once dead weeds have been cleared, the ground can be dug and planted immediately. However, others can remain active in the soil for several months, so always check the manufacturer's specifications before planting ground that has been treated chemically.

The lawn
To rehabilitate a lawn, begin by cutting the grass to within about

2 in (5 cm) of the ground, preferably using a rotary mower, and clear away all grass clippings. Then begin a program of regular mowing, setting the blades according to the height recommended for your type of turf.

Apply a selective weed killer in midspring, when the weeds are actively growing, and then fertilize in late spring and again in early fall. Products that combine fertilizer with herbicide are convenient but less effective, since

▼ **Danger areas** Uneven paving is a hazard. Remove the slabs, dig out the weeds, and treat the area with weed killer before leveling and firming the ground. Stone paving can be relaid on a bed of sand, but a concrete base gives a more stable foundation.

one of the two products must be applied at a less than optimal time.

Moss in a lawn is a symptom of poorly drained, acidic soil. To eradicate it, aerate the soil and apply lime.

In any case, the lawn should be aerated in early fall with a sod-coring or spiked-wheel aerator, and then given a topdressing of organic material such as finely screened, well-rotted garden compost. Add some grass seed to the dressing if there are thin patches. During the next year, follow a standard maintenance program week by week.

If the lawn has been swamped by weeds and moss or the first season's attempt to rehabilitate it has been unsuccessful, consider laying a new one. Kill the existing grass and weeds with an application of a nonselective contact herbicide such as glyphosate, then strip off the old turf. Improve the soil by digging in 3 cu yd (2.3 cu m) of some organic material such as compost per 1,000 sq ft (92 sq m) of surface area, then level and re-sow or resod.

Trees and shrubs

Remove bushes, trees, and hedging plants that are obviously dead, dying, seriously diseased, or overcrowded. Shrubs that have grown too large or are poorly shaped can often be coaxed into shape by cutting them back hard over a couple of seasons, so that a new framework of branches can be established.

Any shrub worth saving should show some vigor in the form of strong, healthy buds. Begin by

▲ Lawn reclamation Renovating a neglected lawn begins with mowing and removal of the resulting debris; the height at which you should mow varies with the type of turf. Apply a selective weed killer in midspring, then fertilize in late spring or early fall. In fall, aerate the lawn with a coring machine and apply screened compost to the surface.

▼ Overgrown apple trees Neglected trees can be helped to yield a good crop again with hard winter pruning over several years. Cut out dead and diseased branches and any that cross and crowd the center; shorten tall branches to strong side shoots; and thin any crowded fruit spurs. Fertilization also helps to revitalize neglected trees.

cutting out all the dead or diseased wood, pruning right back to the ground, and then remove crossing and rubbing branches. Pruning to reduce the height and create a balanced shape should be done in stages over several years.

As with shrubs, neglected trees may have lost their shape or grown too large. Basically sound trees respond well to pruning: cut dead, diseased, damaged, and crossing branches back to the trunk. A pruning saw is the best tool for the job.

Remove the branches in two stages. First, cut off the outer part of the branch that is to be removed, thus reducing the weight. Then, prune away the remainder of the branch just outside the thickened collar of bark at its base. Make your first cut on the underside of the branch, before cutting down from above, in order to sever the branch completely. This approach greatly reduces the risk of tearing the tree bark as the branch falls. You can now prune any remaining stump flush with the branch's collar and trim the edges of the wound neatly with a pruning knife.

Old-timers may recommend the use of "pruning paint" or some wound dressing, arguing that this protects the exposed wood from fungal infection. In fact, these materials slow the

healing process and actually encourage decay.

It's best to prune deciduous trees during the dormant season and evergreens in the spring or early summer. Bracket fungi at the base of a tree usually indicate the presence of core rot, which cannot be treated. Such diseased trees must be removed. Let a professional tree surgeon cut down all but the smallest trees.

Removing tree stumps
Tree stumps should be removed as they may harbor disease spores and insect pests.

You can remove a tree stump by digging it out yourself, a physically demanding job; by having a tree service grind it down below ground level; or by using chemicals to speed decay.
Digging The best time to dig is in clear weather, but when the ground is not too dry. The tools required are a spade, shovel, ax, pickax, and one or more crowbars, depending on the size of the stump. Other useful items are a bow saw, an ax-bladed mattock to dig through matted growth of small roots, and loppers or pruning shears to cut side roots. If the stump is large, you will need a helper when prying it up.

First, clear away vegetation within a 6 ft (1.8 m) radius of the stump to allow room to work and to pile excavated soil.

Take off the surface soil to work out the position of the main roots fanning out from the trunk. Dig away the soil around the main roots to free them, then cut them as close to the main stem as possible. Pry at the roots with a crowbar to find out where they

▲ **Border restoration** A complete overhaul of overgrown beds and borders should be left until the fall. Set aside plants that are worth saving before clearing the bed and digging and fertilizing the soil thoroughly. Replant only healthy young sections of overgrown, divided clumps.

are still holding the tree stump.

When all connections have been severed, pry the stump clear of the hole, then continue to dig out the remaining roots.
Chemicals Potassium nitrate, available in a granular form under trade names such as "root rot" or "stump remover," may be used to speed the decay of tree stumps. When applied according to the product label, it causes a gradual breakdown of the woody tissues that eventually penetrates

to the root tips. This process is slow, however, and it may take months or even a year or more to complete.

Hardscape

Scrutinize man-made features such as fences, walls, and paths. If any need to be repaired or removed, do this at an early stage, when access is easiest. While some repairs, such as relaying a few bricks in a sand-based path or patio, are relatively easy to do yourself, others are labor intensive and require more advanced masonry or carpentry skills. As a rule, major repairs are best left to professionals.

If the condition of a fence is too bad for it to be worth repairing, dig out the posts and dispose of the rotten wood.

If possible, try to preserve old walls — they give a garden character and are expensive to replace. Inspect walls for stability and drainage, checking for poor

construction and damage from falling branches or plants.

Dismantle unstable sections, using a mason's hammer and cold chisel, retaining material for reuse where possible. If the footings are sound, repair the wall by relaying the bricks or stones. The relaid sections must be properly keyed in to the parts of the wall that are still in good condition.

If the whole wall is unsound and a replacement is planned, see if the materials can be used elsewhere before disposing of them.

Paths Old brick or stone paving is often relatively sound. Apply a systemic herbicide to eliminate weeds from the joints, and relay bricks or slabs where necessary.

Broken concrete paving is difficult to repair, so it's best to start afresh. Use a sledgehammer to break up one of the short edges, a crowbar to pry up the paving, and a cold chisel and hammer to break up the fragments into manageable sizes. If there is a footing

of hard-packed rubble beneath the concrete, this can be used as the foundation for a new path.

Check existing patios for uneven flagstones, and pry up any that may trip someone; relay the stones on a fresh, firm bed of sand. Chip away any crumbling edges on concrete paths, and consider extending the area with an "apron" of stone paving, embedded in cement.

Demolish sheds or greenhouses in poor condition, and replace or relocate them as necessary — even if you postpone a replacement, include it in the scale plan.

Ground preparation

To prepare any rough or uneven ground for planting, double-dig

▼ **Semiwilderness** The charm of a "back-to-nature" garden is marred by a greenhouse past redemption. The strawberry netting does not deter the insect pests that hide and breed in clumps of weeds.

▲ **Old-fashioned roses** Old and species roses require only occasional pruning. However, they do need trimming and thinning to allow the air and light to reach them.

▼ **Pruning aesthetics** The rugged profile of this old staghorn sumac (*Rhus typhina*) is picturesque. A skillful pruner will accentuate this look rather than forcing the tree into a symmetrical form.

the soil in fall. Temporarily remove the top layer of soil, then loosen the subsoil another spade-length deep with a fork. Mix some composted organic matter into the topsoil that you removed. Now, replace the topsoil and leave the ground rough to weather during the winter. In spring, level the ground, then dig and fork it over again. Mark out the areas where the lawn, new garden paths, and patio (if any) will be. If you plan a shed or greenhouse, lay the foundations now.

This is a good time to conduct a soil test to determine the soil's acidity or alkalinity and its fertility. The results can have a bearing on the selection of fertilizers and the eventual choice of plants.

With large areas, consider renting a heavy-duty rotary tiller to break up the ground. As this method can chop up and scatter the roots of perennial weeds, eliminate as many as possible beforehand.

It may take years of annual compost application and regular feeding with a general fertilizer to achieve a rich, moisture-retentive and productive soil. In a large garden, it may not be worth improving certain areas of poor soil. Instead, plant them with ivy or other tough ground-cover plants.

EYESORES

Imaginative screening can hide ugly but unavoidable features in or near the garden, plus increase privacy.

▲ **Colorful coverup** In fall a dense curtain of Boston ivy (*Parthenocissus tricuspidata*) envelops a garage in vivid scarlet and crimson.

No matter how well planned and successfully cultivated a garden is, various objects, such as a garage, garbage cans, gas and electricity meters, or a metal cover in the middle of the lawn or patio, can spoil the effect. What's more, constructions outside the garden can spoil the enjoyment of what is inside. A busy road, a railway line, an ugly building, or electricity lines can all be intrusive.

To disguise ugly features or to create an oasis of privacy from the road or from overlooking windows, you can add new structures to the garden, modify existing ones, or devise imaginative planting arrangements to lure the eye away from the offending object.

Planning screening

Before deciding on what and where to plant or build, make an initial survey to ensure that the proposed planting or building will do the job. For this you will need long bamboo canes to indicate likely heights and widths, and someone to help hold the canes as you check the viewing points.

Remember that excessively high or wide screens, whether fences or plants, can be just as unsightly as the object being concealed. If the main view of the eyesore is from a sitting area, you may be able to screen it out with a comparatively small feature — a shrub or small tree planted close to the patio, for example, can block the view from a chair.

If you wish for privacy from your neighbors, but still want to retain the best view of your garden, build a snug sanctuary that is free from prying eyes but open to the view: an arbor decorated with climbing plants or a hedge, wall, or fence erected on three sides will suit the purpose.

Alternatively, consider the patio design. Most people, when building a patio, tend to raise it above the surrounding garden. But if it is sunk by as little as 1 ft (30 cm), it is just as attractive and creates its own sheltered microclimate. It also changes the perspective on the eyesore, possibly eliminating it from view entirely. If it doesn't, a few relatively small shrubs may obscure the offending sight when you are seated and also provide an element of privacy. To block the view from an outdoor seating area more completely, grow tall shrubs or grasses in tubs and position them strategically around the site.

Erecting a pergola over the patio can also screen the sitting area — and you — from view and provide cover at the same time. Still another alternative is to locate the sitting area so that you are looking away from the eyesore. There is no reason why a sitting area should be near the house, if it means looking at something

▼ **Conifer screens** A row of closely planted conifers can be a somber sight. Here, purple-leaved Norway maples (*Acer platanoides* 'Crimson King') provide a pleasant contrast.

unattractive. Make the area next to the house attractive with low shrub plantings, and sit at the other end of the garden to enjoy this more pleasing view.

If this is impractical or impossible, there are still things you can do to improve the situation. Attach an awning above your living room windows to form a "blind," keeping you from seeing above that level when you look out.

Another possibility is to create an attractive feature elsewhere in the garden — for instance, a rock garden or a small pool with a fountain — which will catch the eye and draw it away from the

unsightly view. This distraction will be most effective if it contrasts with its background and surroundings.

To work well, however, the contrast must be noticeable but subtle. The idea is to create an impression without disturbing the balance of the garden. Building a raised planting bed from stone in a brick-dominated garden merely replaces one eyesore with another. On the other hand, a bed constructed from the same bricks as the house, imaginatively planted and well sited, might be distraction enough.

A less expensive and less labor-intensive option is to introduce

contrast through planting. For example, a golden-leaved shrub against a dark yew hedge always draws the eye.

For a more dramatic effect, try installing a statue or pergola. Choose materials and the color scheme carefully. Should the focal point need emphasizing when the garden is in summer bloom, contrast it with the planting. A pale statue or white pergola will blend in with pale flowers instead of standing out, so keep the colors around and behind it bright, or grow a dark red rose up the pergola itself.

It's hard to draw the eye away from a utility box cover or utility

meter that is set in the middle of a lawn. In that case, imagination is your most valuable tool. Construct a pergola over the utility box cover; although the pergola won't cover the eyesore completely, it will draw the eye up and away. Or camouflage a low-lying eyesore by parking something portable over its top, such as a wheelbarrow full of potted plants. If you don't need access to the eyesore, you can hide it with a permanent feature, of course. You could make it the base for a statue or a birdbath, or use it as the foundation for an attractive built-in barbecue.

To hide a more obtrusive feature such as a gas meter, you might surround it with some favorite shrubs, then mulch them — and the offending object — with bark chips, which can be easily brushed aside.

Fences, walls, and hedges

Fences come in a wide range of styles and shades suitable for any garden and provide good visual as well as physical barriers.

Panel or solid fences offer shelter from the wind, creating a milder microclimate in their lee that is suitable for plants of dubious hardiness. Keep in mind, however, that such fences can also block out the sun. And if you wish to add climbing plants, you must provide them with wires to which they may cling.

Open fences are decorative, especially picket and rustic pole fences, and more accommodating to climbing plants. Less attractive ones, such as chain-link types, can be used as supports for twin-ing climbers. The visual result is a solid, though leafy, barrier.

Even without climbing plants, an open fence minimizes the presence of an eyesore outside the garden. Though an open fence doesn't block a view entirely, the fence's symmetrical pattern attracts the eye and breaks up the ugly lines of a distant eyesore. Picket fencing is particularly good at producing this kind of optical illusion.

Wooden lattice (which comes in panels of various sizes) is not strong enough to make a fence by itself, but when mounted on top of a wall or solid fence it increases the height and therefore the screening potential.

Before erecting any form of fence or wall, check the local building codes in case there are restrictions. It is also sensible to mention your plans to your neighbors; they might — if you are lucky — be willing to contribute to the cost.

Walls can provide screening and become ornamental features. They are costly to build, but are long-lasting and require little maintenance. As they retain heat, walls can provide a haven for climbers that might not otherwise prove hardy in your region.

Hedges are the most natural of boundaries. They filter the wind and help to screen out dust as well as noise from a busy road. They can be as tall as you want — depending on the plants you choose and how often you clip them. Evergreens provide a solid barrier all year; deciduous hedges can introduce flowers in spring or summer, or add fall color. Hedges

▲ **Visual deception** High walls and fences frame the leafy outstretched arms of a large tree and shield a multilevel Japanese garden from the outside world. A garden seat at the base of the tree integrates so well that at first glance it is barely noticeable. The success of this type of screening must be balanced against the feeling of confinement it may create and the unavoidable loss of sunlight.

▶ **Utility box cover** The spreading branches of young prostrate junipers planted near a metal plate will eventually extend across the unsightly cover. When access is required, the foliage can be pushed aside without fear of damaging it.

◄ **Clinging ivy** Provided the mortar is sound, variegated or green ivy will rapidly and completely cover architectural eyesores, including drain-pipes. Self-attaching, the ivy can provide a foothold for another climber, such as *Clematis alpina*, which in late spring brightens the evergreen cover with violet-blue flowers and later with silky seed heads.

▼ **Chain-link fencing** Strong and durable but hardly a thing of beauty, chain-link fencing makes an ideal framework for the fast-growing silver-lace vine *(Polygonum aubertii)*. The rampant branches can grow as much as 15 ft (4.5 m) in a season and can quickly conceal unsightly features, hiding them beneath clouds of white or pale pink flowers.

of *Rosa rugosa* or berberis will produce blossoms, fall color, and brightly colored hips or berries in the winter.

Fast-growing hedges and climbers are usually hungry for nutrients. If other plants are grown at their base, regular applications of fertilizer and water are necessary. Hedge plants also require constant attention to prevent them from growing too big. Privet *(Ligustrum)* is a popular hedging plant, but it needs clipping at least three times a year.

Climbing plants

Many annual climbers are suitable for screening sitting areas in summer. Sweet peas *(Lathyrus)*, morning glory *(Ipomoea),* and Chilean glory flower *(Eccremocarpus scaber)* all have attractive flowers. If you want both beauty and usefulness, try the old-fashioned scarlet runner bean *(Phaseolus coccineus)*, which has showy scarlet flowers and edible beans.

More permanent plant screens can be created from deciduous climbers, such as clematis, honeysuckle *(Lonicera),* and hop *(Humulus lupulus)*. For year-round cover choose ivy *(Hedera)*, especially the white- and gold-

variegated forms with different leaf shapes.

All these climbers make superb decorative cover for an ugly outbuilding or the walls of a house, as long as the construction is of masonry. They can be intertwined with a hedge or trained to grow up and over a shabby wall. However, some, such as wisteria, can have intrusive roots, and others, such as ivies, can creep under shingles and damage a roof.

Trees for screening

A tree or a group of trees provides excellent height and foliage cover in the long term. Choosing the type and size of the tree depends as much on the size of the garden as on the eyesore you wish to blot out. Some trees have wide-ranging roots, and care is needed when siting them so as not to damage walls or drains. Willow *(Salix)* is notorious for this.

Deciduous trees are generally more decorative and grow more quickly than evergreens. They are not necessarily dull in winter. Many have attractive colored bark, like the red bark of some maples *(Acer)* or the gold of the yellow willow (*Salix alba* 'Vitellina'); some have bark that peels attractively, like silver Chinese paper birch *(Betula albo-sinensis)* and the paperbark maple *(Acer griseum)*. Still others have convoluted branches, like the dragonclaw willow (*Salix matsudana* 'Tortuosa'), which can distract the eye from any ugly features that lie beyond.

Many trees suitable for screening have the added advantage of blossom. For a spring display, choose a flowering cherry *(Prunus)*, crab apple *(Malus)*, or Judas tree *(Cercis siliquastrum)*. For early summer, try a laburnum. Ornamental cherries and crab apples also provide fall color.

If you decide on an evergreen screen, the first choice may be conifers. Consider your selection carefully, however, for even the very popular Leyland cypresses (× *Cupressocyparis leylandii*) grow to 30 ft (9 m) in 10 years. Apart from obscuring more than you intended and shutting out the sunlight, the large grown tree will probably need an arborist's help to prune it back or remove it — an expensive proposition.

Small to medium-size conifers in attractive colors, from blue-

▲ **Climbing camouflage** Only the downspout from the gutter hints at the water barrel that is hidden behind a screen of variegated ivy. Careful clipping prevents the scrambling stems from creeping under the roof.

green through gray to gold, are eye-catching and have good covering properties. Their shapes are varied — from the narrow columnar *Chamaecyparis lawsoniana* 'Columnaris' to the round-topped *Thuja occidentalis* 'Sunkist.'

Planting conifers in a row is a common method of screening eyesores, but rows can look regimented in an otherwise informal garden. Unless your objective is to shut out the outside world entirely, it is best to arrange conifers in a casual group or to create a display by combining interesting shapes and colors in an island bed with heathers *(Calluna)*.

There are other evergreens besides conifers, such as holly *(Ilex)* or cherry laurel *(Prunus laurocerasus)*. Both can be clipped to form a pleasing shape, and hollies come in variegated forms.

Screening shrubs

Many shrubs eventually grow as tall as small trees. These include blossoming shrubs such as rhododendron, hebe, or hydrangea; variegated foliage shrubs like *Elaeagnus pungens*; or seasonal colored shrubs like sumac *(Rhus)*.

Other tall plants used as screens are bamboos, especially in the South. Arrow bamboo *(Pseudosasa japonica)* grows as high as 15 ft (4.5 m), while hedge bamboo *(Bambusa multiplex)* may grow 20 ft (6 m) high. Bamboos quickly develop into large clumps providing a dense cover, but plant them with caution as many species are extremely invasive.

There are several tall grasses, the largest being *Miscanthus sacchariflorus,* which grows to 10 ft

19

(3 m) high in its second year but is slow to spread sideways. Other tall grasses are pampas grass *(Cortaderia)* and feather grass *(Stipa)*. These die back to the roots in the winter and must be cut back to just above ground level in the spring. They soon grow again to their full height, but the cover that they offer is seasonal.

Screens in the kitchen garden

Runner beans are not the only edible plants that can be used to hide the compost pile or a patch of cabbages; blackberries and raspberries can be trained to grow on wires, or you can plant a row of filberts *(Corylus avellana* or *C. maxima)*. Apple and pear trees, which are often trained to grow along rustic frameworks as espaliers, cordons, or fans, carry spring blossoms and fall fruit.

Pole beans are as prolific as runners and come in green or purple forms. Vining squashes and cucumbers can be trained upward, and some tomato cultivars will grow 4 ft (1.2 m) high.

Herbs are often thought of as small plants, but some tall-growing perennial varieties, such as lovage and bronze fennel, reach 7 ft (2.1 m) or more every year, before dying back in winter.

▲ **Compost hideaway** A box of valuable compost will soon disappear behind a screen of climbing runner beans.

▼ **From eyesore to focal point** Two dead plum trees have been given a new lease on life, as support for *Clematis montana.*

RETAINING WALLS

**Steeply sloping sites are problematic,
but retaining walls and level planting terraces
offer an economical solution.**

Even the smallest and most awkwardly shaped plot can be transformed into a successful and beautiful garden with ingenuity and thoughtful landscaping. Skillful planting can help to disguise and soften an intrusive structure and hard vertical lines. Ornamental features and focal points can draw attention away from a garden's outlines.

Such design devices work well on level lots. However, certain limitations exist if you plan designs for steeply sloping sites, especially if the slope runs toward the house rather than away from it. Major earth moving is generally impractical, so often the best solution is to build one or more retaining walls, with flights of steps linking level terraces with lawns and planting areas.

The small garden described here has one major problematic feature that is nearly impossible to disguise — a high retaining wall, built in red brick to match the house and constructed only a few yards away from the house windows.

The difficulties have been more or less overcome by rich and intense planting. Terraced beds at the highest level overflow with flowering shrubs and perennials pouring over the curving wall; the wall itself is covered with climbers and masked by exuberant planting in the bed below.

The outer perimeter of a brick wall and wooden fences are partly hidden by shrubs and small trees. Pots and containers in all shapes and sizes crowd the lower patio and decorate the small pool area.

The site

The garden is 50 ft (15m) wide and 60 ft (18 m) long. It faces southeast, and being at the top of a hill, it is exposed to winds, although it is protected to some extent by fencing. In winter the lower level is in danger of becoming a frost pocket.

Faced with an oddly situated lot and a markedly abrupt change of level not far from the house windows, the owners of this garden decided to make a strength of the site's peculiarities. The lower garden and the top garden were tackled separately but planted in much the same style, so that they complement each other and unite in effortless profusion at the height of summer.

The soil here is very sandy and free-draining, which is likely to cause great problems in the summer. When the weather is hot, it becomes baked and parched, and soil erosion is a particular danger when heavy rain arrives after a long dry spell. To minimize the risk of washouts, the top beds were divided into a number of shallow terraces edged with railroad ties. Liberal amounts of straw-rich manure and other organic materials were dug into the soil before planting.

▼ **Soil erosion** Close planting in the beds on the upper terrace prevents soil from being washed away over the retaining wall. Evergreen ivy softens the appearance of solid red brick.

A small pool creates a focal point to help relieve the monotony of the long and narrow lower terrace. Concrete paving slabs, large river pebbles, and overspilling plants from the surrounding flower beds hide the edges of the pool.

The retaining wall is successfully masked from the house by a profusion of flowering climbers and perennials that cascade over the brickwork from above and combine with exuberant planting in the bed at its foot. There's a lively intermingling of climbing favorites, such as honeysuckle, clematis, and ivy.

The smooth lawn is in quiet contrast to the dense planting in the beds and creates an illusion of space. The view of the garden and the countryside beyond can be enjoyed from a carefully sited bench on the upper level of the garden.

N

High-rise plantings could be inappropriate in a small, compact garden, but this slender, tall conifer *(Chamaecyparis lawsoniana* 'Ellwoodii') and the erect Japanese cherry *(Prunus serrulata* 'Amanogawa') balance the dense low-level planting without taking up too much ground space.

Design features

The garden has a number of interesting and attractive design features, including the terraces and the high brick wall, whose severity is softened by a gentle curve. The irregular steps, with risers alternately three and two bricks deep, may be disconcerting to climb, but look charming; at the top of the steps is a birdbath.

The lower terrace features a small pool surrounded by large pebbles and concrete paving slabs. Triangular in shape, this pool acts as a focal point and helps to break up the terrace garden's long and narrow rectangular lines, which might otherwise seem relentless.

A patio and a path of concrete slabs provide structure and a uniform background to this part of the garden. A flight of steps winds around the retaining wall to the garden's upper level. A wooden bench stands just a couple of yards away.

The open grass area helps to prevent this part of the garden from seeming too overcrowded — even in the smallest garden, it is important to create areas of uninterrupted calm.

The planting

By early summer, the long curving wall is entirely hidden by climbers and shrubs planted at its base. The vigorous climbing hydrangea *(Hydrangea anomala petiolaris)*, with flat heads of white flowers, has pride of place. Nearby is the five-leaved *Akebia quinata*, equally vigorous and notable for its small and fragrant reddish-purple flowers in late spring.

The variegated ivy *Hedera helix* 'Goldheart' appears in several places, tumbling over the wall and mingling with honeysuckle and clematis. Knotweed *(Polygonum affine)* has spikes of pink flowers all through the summer; its lance-shaped leaves turn rusty brown in fall and winter.

Four types of clematis flourish on the wall — rich purple *Clematis viticella*, shell-pink 'Hagley Hybrid,' deep lavender 'Countess of Lovelace' (double-flowered in summer, single in fall), and 'Mrs. N. Thompson,' which bears violet flowers, each with a pink stripe.

A Chinese wisteria *(Wisteria sinensis)* covers the boundary wall. Surprisingly, it is planted in a large container, together with a hydrangea. Daphnes are featured in the long bed below the wall; of note is a large specimen of sweet-scented *Daphne odora* 'Aureomarginata,' with pale purple flowers and white-edged leaves, and the evergreen garland flower *(D. cneorum* 'Eximia'), which is rose-pink and also highly scented.

▼ **Sun trap** Sheltered from the wind by a high retaining wall, the lower terrace is planted with sun-loving shrubs, hardy perennials, and bedding plants.

The small pool is surrounded by rich planting, including marsh marigolds *(Caltha palustris)*, deep red lobelias *(Lobelia* 'Queen Victoria'), and large-flowered yellow monkey flower *(Mimulus)*. Honesty *(Lunaria annua)* self-seeds everywhere, as do hellebores, especially the Christmas rose *(Helleborus niger)* and the Lenten rose *(H. orientalis)*, which bears purple, pink, or white blossoms in early spring. The bright red calyxes of Chinese lanterns *(Physalis alkekengi)* provide splashes of color throughout the garden in fall.

Rock roses *(Cistus)* blossom nearly everywhere — this garden is ideal for them as they thrive in dry, hot, sunny places. Although sandy, the soil is quite acidic, allowing miniature rhododendrons and azaleas to grow in the bed above the wall.

Two trees immediately stand out in the top garden — a hybrid Japanese cherry tree *(Prunus serrulata* 'Amanogawa'), with its upright pencil shape, greenish-bronze young leaves, and fragrant shell-pink flowers, and *Chamaecyparis lawsoniana* 'Ellwoodii.' To balance these tall, slender shapes is a low-growing spreading *Magnolia stellata* 'Rosea' with white, pink-flushed flowers.

The shallow terraced beds edged with railroad ties contain a great variety of flowering plants and small shrubs, including hebe, coronilla, and osmanthus. The main bed is bordered by an entire bed of sun roses *(Helianthemum)*, including orange-scarlet *H.* 'Fire Dragon' and soft pink *H.* 'Wisley Pink.'

A prostrate juniper near the steps requires frequent clipping to prevent it from spreading too far. The rear fence is clothed with some reliable and attractive shrubs: hardy cotoneaster, which bears white flowers in early summer, followed by red berries; *Hibiscus syriacus* 'Woodbridge,' with its rose-crimson carmine-centered blooms; and *Kerria japonica,* with golden yellow buttercup-like flowers.

Behind the bench is a tall, yellow-flowered, summer-blooming broom *(Cytisus)*. Purple broom also grows in this top garden, and *Genista lydia,* an excellent dwarf shrub, produces golden flowers in late spring and early summer.

▲ **High views** Magnificent views of the surrounding countryside are seen from the upper terrace. The curved lines of encircling beds and borders release the garden from its rectangular confines.

▼ **Prefabricated pool** A miniature pool breaks the rigid shape of the lower terrace. Ringed by white pebbles and edged with water-loving plants, the pool becomes a striking focal point.

A TERRACED GARDEN

Despite steep slopes, poor soil, and a northern exposure, this small yard has been turned into a terraced garden filled with inspired planting.

This small north-facing garden lies on a steep slope and receives continuous sun only near the rear wall. The two redeeming features are the shelter afforded by the high, red brick boundary walls and the wind barrier created by nearby sheds and garages, as well as the huge holly and yew trees. Such shelter permits the cultivation of a wide variety of plants, including many that are of questionable winter hardiness in this zone; however, the lack of sunlight limits the choice. A lush garden has been created using foliage plants, with bright color coming from shade-tolerant flowering shrubs, climbers, perennials, and ground-cover plants.

The steep slope has been transformed into three level terraces linked by flights of steps. The upper terrace, bounded by a high wall, enjoys the best of the available sun and light.

The garden lies on a quick-draining sand ridge. The original soil was thin and poor until liberal amounts of manure, spent mushroom compost, and slow-acting organic fertilizers were dug in to increase its depth and add to its organic and mineral content. The result is a fertile garden, densely planted with clematises, ferns, ivies, and alpines.

The lower level
Facing due north, a greenhouse is attached to the rear of the house. Although it receives only morning sun for most of the year, this structure is home to many tender plants, including trailing staghorn ferns, climbing *Hoya carnosa,* and *Plumbago auriculata*.

The greenhouse opens out onto a paved terrace furnished with raised beds, many containers, and a huge terra-cotta pot holding a *Clematis alpina*. The terrace is bordered on one side by a high brick wall draped with climbing roses, such as the shell-pink, thornless, shade-tolerant, and sweet-scented *Rosa* 'Kathleen Harrop,' and with various clematis cultivars, including *Clematis* 'Captain Thuilleaux,' with large creamy pink and carmine flowers.

A tripod of scented honeysuckle towers above a low stone wall adjoining the greenhouse. Opposite are raised beds, partly surrounding a small pool complete with clumps of pink water lilies. Ferns and purple-spotted toad lilies *(Tricyrtis)* at the edges thrive in the cool, moist shade.

Ivies flourish in cool, shady

▼ **Lower level** In almost constant shade, this terrace is an oasis of greenery, from arching ferns and trailing ivies to climbing honeysuckles. Pots of alpines add summer color.

places, and the raised beds on the lower level are filled with them. Throughout the garden, some 90 different varieties of ivy are used to soften and enliven the extensive brickwork and stone foundations. They climb up walls, spread to form ever-increasing ground cover, and trail from pots.

Various containers occupy the floor at ground level. Large pots hold hostas and other plants such as golden bamboos, whose invasive roots need restriction; shallow half pots house alpines.

The foundations of an old storage shed now support a delightful small fernery. The bricks from the floor have been reused to form raised beds, and the small space is crammed with different species, including spleenwort (*Asplenium*) and Australian fern (*Doodia*). Little club mosses (*Selaginella*) run along the base of the lower wall. The fernery gets a little afternoon sun, but is lightly shaded by the honeysuckle and clematis above.

A brick path runs from the front of the greenhouse and along the fernery; it is flanked on one side by a low stone wall that sprouts spleenwort ferns. Three stony troughs along the base of the wall hold a variety of alpine plants, especially saxifrages and campanulas. Though all three troughs look like solid stone, only one is the genuine article. The others, a zinc basin and a shiny white porcelain sink, have been

▲ **Alpine troughs** Large weathered containers hold mature collections of saxifrages and miniature gray-leaved hebes. Spleenwort ferns find a foothold in the wall, below shallow pans of evergreen sempervivums and sedums.

▼ **Alpine slope** Rising gently toward a retaining wall, the dense planting, top-dressed with gravel, disguises the sloping site. Boundary walls are clothed with ivies and clematises, and mosses fill cracks in the paving stones.

covered with a sticky rubberized adhesive and then coated with a mixture of peat moss, sand, and cement. The result, over the years, is a trough that looks like weathered stone. Each container is filled with a free-draining mixture of good soil and grit to provide the plants with a perfect growing environment.

On the opposite side of the path is a double-tiered bed of peat-enriched soil good for acid-loving plants. These narrow beds support spring bulbs, such as bright yellow *Adonis amurensis;* summer-flowering corydalis; fall-flowering gentians; late-winter- or early-spring-flowering primulas; and a number of dwarf rhododendrons.

The second level
The path continues up some steps to reach the second level, which is a broad platform running the width of the garden. The steps lead through a large tubular steel archway covered with ornamental quince *(Chaenomeles)* for spring color and the creamy apricot, heavily scented rose 'Gloire de Dijon.'

At the back of the garden large stately urns, visible from the house, function as impressive

focal points. Sited near the steps, these are set off by a semi-circular boxwood hedge. Close to the urns, a raised brick bed has been planted entirely with white plants, including *Phlox maculata* 'Omega,' monardas, polemoniums, and musk mallow.

Two upright barberries and a pair of dwarf yews help to give perspective to the scene beyond the archway. To convey a feeling of space, plants near the rear wall tend to be pale or subtly colored — light pinks, mauves,

▲ **Second level** Bold planting dominates the wide platform, which is entered through an archway of clematises and roses. A lone Japanese cherry *(Prunus serrulata)* adds height to the beds and is smothered with pink-budded, pure white flower clusters in the spring.

▼ **Containers of plants** On the lower terrace, pots and urns are filled with foliage plants that thrive in the cool shade. They include golden-leaved fuchsias, silver-gray dianthus, ornamental grasses, and a yellow-leaved hydrangea.

and grays — while those nearer the house are brighter reds, oranges, and yellows.

To the left and beyond the arch, in an area of shade and dappled sunlight, a sunken brick-lined bed has been converted into a bog garden, supporting bog primulas and moisture-loving ferns. Nearby is a large white-flowered hydrangea and two small crab apple trees. *Malus* 'Golden Hornet' has dense clusters of pink flowers in spring and bright yellow fruit in fall.

The third level
A dark green upright yew marks a flight of paving stone steps that leads to the top level and the rear wall. In this area — the only truly sunny part of the garden — several normally bushy shrubs such as rosemary, senecio, and spindle tree *(Euonymus)* have been carefully trained in fan shapes up against the red brick wall.

A central flight of steps leads

◄ **Strawberry planter** A terra-cotta pot planted with dainty-flowered alpine pinks and rosettes of sempervivum adds a splash of warm color to a tracery of green.

PLANTED STEPS

1 Four-leaf clover *(Trifolium repens 'Purpurascens')*
2 Common bugle *(Ajuga reptans 'Burgundy Glow')*
3 Sweet violet *(Viola odorata)*
4 Garden pink *(Dianthus x allwoodii)*
5 Japanese barberry *(Berberis thunbergii 'Atropurpurea Nana')*
6 Stars-of-Persia *(Allium christophii)*
7 Garden pink *(Dianthus)*
8 English daisy *(Bellis perennis)*
9 Golden English ivy *(Hedera helix 'Buttercup')*
10 Bellflower *(Campanula portenschlagiana)*
11 Bleeding heart *(Dicentra eximia)*
12 Alpine toadflax *(Linaria alpina)*
13 Tree peony *(Paeonia lutea)*
14 Cerastium *(Cerastium alpinum)*
15 Nemesia *(Nemesia strumosa)*
16 Miniature hybrid rose
17 Violet *(Viola spp.)*
18 Antennaria *(Antennaria)*
19 English lavender *(Lavandula angustifolia)*
20 Lamb's ears *(Stachys byzantina)*
21 Variegated English ivy
22 Dead nettle *(Lamium)*
23 Hybrid tea rose
24 Twinspur *(Diascia barberae hybrid)*
25 Blue fescue *(Festuca glauca)*
26 Cranesbill *(Geranium ibericum)*
27 Rosemary *(Rosmarinus officinalis)*
28 Garden geranium
29 Cranesbill *(Geranium)*
30 Masterwort *(Astrantia major)*
31 Japanese spindle tree *(Euonymus japonica)*
32 Russian olive *(Elaeagnus)*
33 Clematis hybrid
34 Common white jasmine *(Jasminum officinale)*

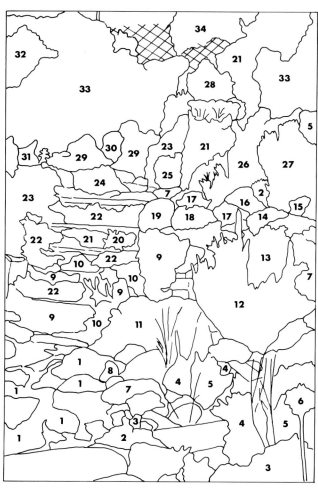

ground level. It supports four species of berberis, gray-leaved thalictrum, purple-leaved cimicifuga, callicarpa with bright purple flowers and fruit, and a yellow-leaved *Choisya ternata.*

In winter the flowers of witch hazel *(Hamamelis),* wintersweet *(Chimonanthus),* and *Viburnum × bodnantense* provide color and a delicious sweet scent.

A variegated cut-leaved shrub *Acanthopanax* is trained as a single-trunked "standard." The top growth is pruned back hard in late winter to admit enough light for an underplanting of spring bulbs. Ivy is used as background and support for an elegant bright red *Clematis texensis.*

Various yellow-flowered and foliage plants also thrive here in partial shade. They include phygelius, golden lamium for ground cover, daisylike golden marguerite *(Anthemis tinctoria* 'Mrs. E.C. Buxton'), and yellow lilylike montebretias *(Crocosmia).*

The shrubbery also includes spring bulbs — snowdrops, blue scillas, dwarf daffodils, and fritillaries. Planted in the bed and spilling over the paving stones are some black- and green-leaved *Ophiopogon planiscapus* plants, which resemble small tufted grasses but are in fact members of the lily family.

up to the back boundary wall, while a third set of steps curves slightly to end in a miniature alpine scree area. Narrow beds are crowded with sun-loving pinks, lavender cotton, marjoram, lavender, and thyme. Between the paving stones, and alongside and spilling over the steps, is an array of plants, ranging from cactuslike cobweb houseleek *(Sempervivum arachnoideum)* to small, strongly aromatic Corsican mint.

The top right corner is dominated by pink-flowered plants such as everlasting sweet pea, *Jasminum × stephanense, Clematis* 'Ernest Markham,' pink Japanese anemones, the pink bourbon rose 'Louise Odier,' and a purple-leaved ornamental grapevine.

Raised shrubbery
Although of modest proportions, the bed at the rear of the garden houses a variety of shrubs and perennials with irregular shapes, which break up the view from

▲ **Water nymphs** A fountain in the pool on the lower terrace sends soft sprays of water over moisture-loving ferns. Also thriving in the damp soil are the arching spikes of bleeding heart *(Dicentra formosa).* Their color will be echoed by the water lilies when they bloom.

▼ **Ground-cover plants** In moist ground touched by sunlight, yellow-flowered evergreen saxifrages thrive and spread readily. A summer-flowering garden pansy bears its bicolored yellow and purple-brown blooms for many months and is excellent for underplanting.

CHANGES IN LEVEL

**Flat, uninspiring gardens can be
given new beauty, character, and interest by
introducing some changes in level.**

Very few gardens are truly flat — that is, perfectly level, not sloping in any direction. Even if a garden appears flat, it still probably slopes evenly over a wide area. Gardens with wide expanses of lawn can be beautiful, but they can also be predictable and unexciting. Natural-looking changes in level can help add interest.

In the days of large country estates, when labor was cheap, massive excavation and stonework created changes in level on a grand scale. The purpose was to

create an impressive setting for the house and an attractive view from it. Level changes in an ordinary garden are more modest, but the purposes are similar and the result just as pleasing.

Natural or artificial
Some gardens already have obvious level changes — natural formations such as steep banks, gentle slopes, or rocky outcrops. The usually irregular form of natural level changes gives a garden unique character and can often

suggest the best position for beds, borders, and a lawn.

You can enhance natural level changes with plants: add ground cover to natural slopes that are too steep to mow; site a tree on top of a hill; grow water-loving plants on the steep banks of a

---

▼ **Tiers of terraces** A magnificent banked effect has been created in this small garden by adding tiers of raised beds and retaining walls, profusely planted with colorful azaleas.

▲ **Formal beds** Even a slight change in level can be effective. This small raised bed keeps soil and plants well above the surrounding paved area and creates a neat and tidy look.

◄ **Flights of steps** On all but the gentlest of slopes, steps of harmonious materials are essential as links between different levels.

stream; or tuck alpine plants into a rocky outcrop. Or you can use more durable materials: place a few large boulders on a natural slope to suggest a rocky outcrop, or form an exhilarating "mountain" path with stepping stones.

In many gardens a more formal treatment is appropriate. Attempts at creating a naturalistic landscape behind a townhouse, for example, may look artificial. Besides, you may simply prefer the regularity of a formal landscape. Here, the changes in level may include ramps, steps, retaining walls, raised planting beds, and sunken patios and pools.

Natural-looking artificial level changes include sloping banks, extending down to a garden boundary, driveway, path, or pavement; ditches; earthen mounds made from excavated materials from house foundations; or earthwork berms raised to cut down noise from passing traffic. Existing mounds, slopes, and banks can be sodded or planted with low shrubs, or even serve as the base for a children's play area.

Benefits of changes in level

Creating level changes often has a practical purpose, but it can also greatly enhance the appearance of a garden. In a large garden, generous level changes add an element of mystery, deliberately obstructing a complete view of the garden from any one point. (Hiding the house from certain viewpoints in the garden is important if you want a "wilderness" effect.) A mound, especially if topped with planting, can camouflage an unpleasant view, such as a nearby building, garden shed, or compost pile.

Level changes can define space, showing the boundaries of a patio area, for example, or the end of a property. They can also separate a flower garden from a vegetable patch or mark the change from a formal garden to a more informal area.

Because the general feeling of a garden is horizontal — sky, horizon, lawn, and rooftops — strongly vertical level changes naturally become focal points. A series of level changes, such as a long flight of steps with several landings or a series of stepped raised beds, creates a sense of movement and rhythm.

In a small garden, precise level changes — a raised bed, steps, or ramp — may define the garden's layout. In awkwardly shaped lots, such as a long, thin garden, raised areas can disguise or improve the overall shape.

Raised beds and banks add instant "maturity" to new plantings. Small shrubs and trees that appear modest at ground level gain stature from their borrowed height. Raised beds are easier to tend than ground-level ones and, in the case of heavy clay soils, provide better drainage.

Lastly, level changes can create shelter and a feeling of enclosure and privacy. A sunken sitting area or one at ground level surrounded by raised beds can become a delightful hideaway.

Formality or informality

If you inherit a garden with level changes, it's important to make

▲ **Planting terraces** Different types of building materials can work together successfully. Natural stone has been used to edge a low raised bed and in a rock garden above. The two are linked by steps of pale concrete paving slabs set on brick risers.

the most of them. But if your garden is nearly flat, you can start from scratch and create your own alterations.

Decide first whether you want a formal or informal effect. Formal level changes can be carried out simply by using earth and lawn, or they can be built of brick, stone, concrete, or wood. Old railroad ties are a popular material; if they aren't available, you can achieve a similar effect with landscape timbers pressure-treated with a preservative.

By using the same construction material — brick, for instance — at various levels, both horizontally and vertically, for paths, walls, steps, ramps, and patios, it is possible to create a unified effect, which is especially valuable in a small garden. You can also use stone or concrete blocks for low-level retaining walls, a patio and path, stepping stones, and the treads and risers of steps.

Informal level changes require subtle modeling of the earth if they are to look natural. What

already exists — in the garden and in the surrounding landscape — should affect the design. In broad, flat landscapes, for example, a level change of 2 ft (60 cm) over a wide area can look quite convincing. Generally, mounds that are slightly convex at the top and concave at the base look more natural, as well as being more stable, than sharply angled ones. The actual gradient depends on the design of the mound and the type of soil, but gentle slopes are easier on the eye and more "believable" than steep slopes. They are also easier to mow.

The smaller the garden, the more likely it is that formal, geometric level changes are the right choice. Informal changes in

of a rock garden, and when digging footings for a patio, try to create a surrounding ring of raised beds. When terracing a slope, try to create the new levels through an equal combination of cutting and filling.

Calculating cut and fill can be complicated, especially where slopes over a fairly large area are involved, but a good rule of thumb for equal-size, flat level changes is that the difference in finished levels is double the depth of soil removed. For example, if you remove 1 ft (30 cm) from one area, and spread it evenly over an adjacent area of equal size, the difference in levels will be 2 ft (60 cm).

If you keep the original level in nearby areas, you will have three

▲ **Raised beds** High-level planting beds can serve dual purposes: as level changes they are visually attractive, and practically they are ideal for gardeners with physical disabilities.

▶ **Drainage provision** Drainpipes and weep holes have been constructed at regular intervals in a retaining wall. At the lower level, rainwater on the patio drains away through a gutter.

level, such as irregularly shaped mounds, should have a simple design; those that twist or seem contorted look unnatural.

Practical considerations

Plan any major project carefully, since it will almost always involve a great deal of effort and expense — professional advice, contractors, and rented machinery are likely to be needed. Note, too, that the garden will be disrupted for some time: filled areas, for example, depending on their depth and how well the soil was packed during construction, may take 6 months to a year to settle.

It is easier if you can obtain the soil needed for filling from your own garden, by balancing your filling with a similar amount of excavation. Buying clean fill is expensive, as is paying to have excavated material hauled away. If the only access to the garden is through the house itself (a common situation in city gardens), the project can turn into a prolonged nightmare. Try to combine compatible projects. Use material excavated from the site of a pool to raise the foundation

levels, and more scope for creativity. Or, by concentrating the excavated soil in a smaller area — such as a surrounding raised bed or terrace — you could have a greater level change and, with the increased depth of topsoil, an ideal home for plants. If you are excavating soil for the foundations of a patio or terrace, be sure to take into account the quantity of gravel or crushed rock you must add as a base for the pavement.

When digging, it is important to keep the topsoil — usually darker in color — separate from the subsoil. Topsoil is more difficult than subsoil to compact and takes longer to settle, but it is fertile and essential if you are creating an earth mound, hill, or slope that will be planted when it

is finished. You'll need a layer of topsoil at least 4-6 in (10-15 cm) deep for sod or herbaceous plantings, and at least double that for deep-rooted shrubs and trees.

Whether raising or lowering levels, before you set spade to soil be sure to check the location of waterlines, gas and electric lines, drains, and sewers. The presence of such utilities may force you to redraw plans. If the proposed change affects a garden wall, exposing its foundation may be visually as well as structurally unfortunate, and piling great weights of soil against it could make it collapse.

If there are established plants where you intend to change the levels, you should lift the plants the preceding spring, heel them in elsewhere, and then replant after the project's completion.

Surprisingly, large trees such as sugar maples are among the plants most sensitive to level changes. The addition of just an inch or two of clay soil over the roots may kill such a seemingly robust giant. When raising the soil level substantially, surround the tree with a well filled with crushed stone. Before filling around this, lay down radiating spokes of drainage tile covered with more crushed rock. Run the tiles to the edge of the branches' reach, ending each spoke with a

▲ **Running water** An artificial stream flowing down a steep bank appears as a natural feature. Boulders and flat rocks break the incline and turn it into an arresting focal point.

bell tile that reaches up to the soil's new surface.

Excavation around a tree is even more troublesome since most of the roots run within a foot of the soil's surface. If much soil is to be removed, it is generally best to remove the tree.

Soil and drainage
A common mistake in do-it-yourself gardens is to build retaining walls that are too weak to take the thrust of soil over a period of time. A retaining wall more than 3 ft (90 cm) high should be designed professionally, and lower ones need masonry 9 in (23 cm) thick. Building the wall at a slant against the soil helps strengthen it and can be a design feature as well. Weep holes for relieving water pressure against retaining walls are vital.

The types of soil, subsoil, and bedrock can affect the cost and success of a design. As a rule, the angle of repose of soil — the angle at which it remains stable without being retained — is 35°. This is roughly a 1-in-3 slope; a ground area 3 ft (90 cm) wide is needed to

go up 1 ft (30 cm) in height, and that much again to get back down, without any level area at the top — rather like a soil pyramid. However, this would look steep and be difficult to walk up; a 1-in-12 slope is the maximum for a ramp used for walking.

If you are lowering levels, remember that water seeks the lowest level. Low-lying patios will need drains of some sort and perhaps a dry well. (Lowering the ground in an area with a high water table can create an instant unwanted pool.) Building a slope toward the house will also necessitate a drain or at least a swale to divert the runoff — in heavy

downpours water runs off the soil surface before it can be absorbed.

Planting levels
You can create an impression of altered levels with carefully graduated planting, much like a stage setting — put short plants in front and the tallest in back. When this works, it can be very effective, but there are snags. Unless you use evergreens or densely woody shrubs, the truth will be revealed in winter. You really need a garden that goes back a fair distance to carry out the illusion, and the trick works well only from one viewpoint. You won't get the same effect looking

▲ **"Natural" stairway** Neatly trimmed turf laps here at the edges of risers fashioned from rough poles. Serviceable yet informal, such a flight of steps harmonizes well with the natural look of many modern gardens.

down on the garden from an upstairs window, or from the far end of the garden looking back.

Another way of creating visual level changes in a completely flat garden is to plant an island bed with trees and shrubs of widely varying heights. Not only does this screen — and so add mystery to — various parts of the garden, but it also becomes a focal point.

COVERING BANKS

**Banks and steps, in the sun or shade, can be
transformed from problem areas into attractive
features, clothed in vibrant colors.**

One of the simplest ways to cover a bank is to grass it over. This is suitable for a formal area, but large uneven slopes can be difficult to mow and, if at all steep, dangerous. Yet, certainly, some sort of coverage is essential to prevent soil erosion from a bank. Luckily, in addition to turf, there are many plants that will hold the soil in place — and bring character and color to slopes and banks.

On an open site, use easy-to-grow rock garden plants for an eye-catching display. Colorful rock roses *(Helianthemum)*, for example, are ideal for covering a dry, sunny bank. Up to 1 ft (30 cm) high, these spreading evergreen shrublets — some with silvery gray foliage — are covered with a continuous display of flowers in early summer and midsummer. Trim them back hard after flowering, and they will frequently produce yet another floral show in late summer and early fall. They come in shades of yellow, orange, pink, red, and white.

In regions mostly free of frost, plant some of their taller and larger-flowered relatives, the cistuses, to make the bank more interesting. Sageleaf cistus *(Cistus salviifolius)* is a drought-resistant wide-spreading shrub. It grows only 2 ft (60 cm) high but spreads to 6 ft (1.8 m), bearing big crops of yellow-centered white flowers in late spring.

The smaller lavender cotton *(Santolina chamaecyparissus)* is another sun-loving shrub with silvery foliage that provides a good foil for other plants.

The 9 in (23 cm) high *Campanula poscharskyana* forms a wide-spreading clump in semishade, topped with sprays of starry lavender-blue flowers from summer to fall. By this time, the pink pokerlike flowers of the mat-forming knotweed *(Polygonum affine)* are in full bloom; they combine well with white-flowered campanulas. For vertical interest, use the arching growth of the cream-edged leaves of blue-flowered *Vinca major* 'Variegata.'

Yellow- or white-variegated ivies look decorative covering a shady bank. For extra color during the bleaker months of the year, plant winter jasmine *(Jasminum nudiflorum)* to cascade down the slope. Its yellow flowers open as early as January to enhance the yellow-variegated ivies.

Steps are often an integral part of banks, and unless the garden is very formal, they look more natural if a few plants are allowed to grow on or over them. *Erigeron karvinskianus* is a small Mexican daisy whose white to pale pink flowers appear from late spring until the first frost. Once established, it will create a charming picture by self-seeding in cracks and crevices. A suitable partner is *Campanula portenschlagiana*, with its sprays of starry blue flowers.

◄ **Sunny bank** In late spring a carpet of color sweeps over the gentle contours of a sunny bank. Deep purple *Aubrieta deltoidea* contrasts well with golden *Aurinia saxatilis*, beneath the arching sprays of *Cytisus x praecox* 'Allgold.'

▲ **Carpeting shrubs** On a steep bank, the sharp outline of a long flight of steps is partly hidden by the arching semievergreen branches of a prostrate cotoneaster. The pinkish springtime flowers are insignificant, but the red fall fruits are brilliant.

◄ **Rocky outcrops** Grass is an impossibility on steep and stony slopes that have thin, dry soil, but true alpines will feel at home. Perennials, such as the mat-forming 6 in (15 cm) high aubrieta in all its different shapes and tints, form vibrant carpets of color. The dazzling array is toned down with the pure white of wall rock cress (*Arabis caucasica*).

◀ **A flight of flowers** A partially shaded bank has been cut into a series of shallow planting terraces. In early spring it comes alive with the jewellike flowers of naturalized bulbs, including the early-blooming *Crocus tomasinianus*, winter aconites *(Eranthis hyemalis),* and snowdrops *(Galanthus nivalis).*

Scattered between the spring-flowering bulbs are the handsome silver-marbled leaves of the hardy cyclamen *(Cyclamen hederifolium).* This, too, has naturalized itself, and in late summer and fall it will cover the terraces with its nodding rose-pink blooms.

▶ **Heaths and heathers** A bank with acid soil is the ideal spot for these moorland plants. Both heaths *(Erica)* and heathers *(Calluna)* make an excellent weed-smothering evergreen cover. The 2 ft (60 cm) tall, pink fall-blooming *Calluna vulgaris* 'H.E. Beale' is matched by the mauve-lilac flower spikes and grassy evergreen leaves of *Liriope muscari.* In the foreground, *Hebe pinguifolia* 'Pagei' provides a silver-gray foil.

◄ **Shady steps** However attractive the material, an extensive flight of steps always looks better when its edges are softened by plants. Ferns thrive in the shade — here, in midsummer the distinctive evergreen hart's tongue *(Asplenium scolopendrium)* and its wavy-edged cultivar 'Undulatum' are partnered by the fruiting spikes of *Arum italicum,* many of which have turned a brilliant red. Towering above the ferns and arums are Turk's cap lilies *(Lilium martagon),* with dark red, pink, and white blooms. Arums bring additional interest in spring with their pale yellow spathes and again in winter with their spear-shaped, marbled leaves.

► **Streamside bank** Covered with gravel to improve drainage, the natural contours of this streamside bank have been used to create a sloping rock garden where alpine plants, such as pink-flowered *Saponaria ocymoides* and thrift, flourish. Giving year-round interest are dwarf evergreen conifers — at the back a dense, spreading spruce *(Picea abies* 'Nidiformis'), which reaches a height of only 16 in (40 cm) after 10 years, and in the foreground, rich dark green *Pinus nigra* 'Hornibrookiana.'

GARDENING ON ROCK

**A sloping hillside, studded with outcrops
or boulders, forms the perfect natural setting
for colorful alpine plants.**

It is ironic that people try hard to create a natural-looking rock garden on perfectly flat, flawless lots and rarely succeed, while genuinely rocky slopes and outcrops are often looked on as defects to be corrected. Short of dynamiting the rocks and building earthworks, the best solution for a rocky, sloping garden site is to accept the terrain as it is and use it as the starting point for a unique natural rock garden.

The site

The garden described here is situated on an exposed hilly site and surrounds a traditionally styled stone house and outbuildings. There is a noticeable slope across the lot, and large outcrops of water-worn limestone are concentrated in the highest corner. The climate is coastal with hot and often dry summers and mild, usually frost-free winters.

The owners wanted a garden filled with colorful, undemanding plants that would look after themselves. They planned to keep maintenance to a minimum and to create a level, sunny, and sheltered sitting area, as well as leaving space for paving and a lawn. Some privacy was essential.

The massive rocky outcrop called for an informal approach. Because the rock abuts the house, the design incorporates both natural and artificial elements.

The design

The rocky outcrop remains the main theme and focal point of this new layout, with paving and steps designed to suggest an extension of exposed natural bedrock. By means of cutting and filling — leveling the ground into terraces — part of the slope has been transformed into relatively level lawns. A curving but level sitting area rimmed by an informal stone edging hugs the house.

An unusual path with wide, shallow steps, made of stone risers and sand treads, curves gently down from the terrace, then straightens out to meet the front gate. Along one side of the path a low drystone retaining wall supports a lawn; another drystone wall along the road serves not

---

▼ **Rocky path** A constructed path appears as a natural extension of the exposed bedrock. Made from shallow stone risers and treads of sand, the path curves gently from the front gate to the level sitting area and is dotted with maritime alpine plants.

▲ ◀ **Color patches** Naturalized tulips, perennials, and annuals form swaths of bright color between the honey-colored limestone rocks. The annual pot marigold (*Calendula officinalis*) thrives on the poorest of soils, flowering continuously from late spring onward and leaving behind numerous self-sown seedlings.

▲ **Grassy slopes** Deep-rooted, drought-resistant grasses cover the areas on either side of the path and form lawns along the boundary wall. Grass roots bind the shallow soil and prevent it from washing down the hillside. Informal clumps of spring bulbs and rock plants spill over the steps and grass.

◀ **Alpine meadow** Large outcrops of water-worn rock form the backbone of the garden. Low alpines and sprawling succulents spread a carpet between the rocks and around an Irish heath (*Erica erigena*), which thrives in this mild coastal climate.

only to hold back the soil but also to provide privacy. Stepped dry-stone walls also mark the boundary with neighboring gardens.

Rocks and stones
The usual advice on building a new rock garden from scratch is to use local stone — it looks natural and cuts transport costs. But some types of rock encourage plant life more than others. Slate and granite, for example, are too heavy and dense for moisture and plant roots to penetrate.

Here, the rocky outcrop could not be more local or blend more naturally into the landscape. It is a medium-density limestone that is ideal for rock gardens, as it is porous enough for plant roots and moisture to penetrate while the roots keep cool. Hard limestones of the dolomitic type, or very soft

ones, such as chalk or caliche, are less suitable.

The soft, light color and sculptural quality of limestone — caused by moving water, weathering, and geological buckling and tilting — give it a particularly strong character. The crevices slowly collect grit and organic debris, and provide ideal nursery beds for self-seeding rock plants. This is a natural process that can be speeded up by filling natural depressions in the rock with a mixture of soil and grit.

Rough-hewn drystone retaining walls blend well with the rocky outcrop and offer additional homes for a wide range of plants.

Variety of plants
Most of the plants in this garden are fairly common, but they are

enhanced by their extraordinary setting. Like the stonework, the planting slips easily from the formal to the natural. In late spring there are single red and yellow tulips growing in random clusters among the rocks, while a more formal row of pristine yellow tulips marks the boundary of the front garden.

Although the main focus is on dwarf rock garden plants, there are also bulbs, perennials, annuals, shrubs, and two horse chestnut trees planted here. Tough all-purpose perennials adapted to coastal conditions include clumps of fennel, the late-summer flowering montebretia, and pink and white mallows.

The gentle maritime climate, full sun, and well-drained gritty soil allow plants to thrive that would quickly succumb in wetter,

An area in front of the house has been leveled and turned into a sunny and sheltered patio. Grass is allowed to grow between the paving slabs, which are bedded on sand, without any mortar.

Perennial and annual rock garden plants spill from every cranny in the limestone outcrop. Self-sown seedlings jostle for space, nutrients, and water in the shallow depressions in the rocks.

The rough-hewn blocks of the buildings and garden walls were cut from local stone and look like a natural extension of the rocky site. Drystone walls provide additional homes for rock garden plants.

The steps are made of stone risers and sand treads—unusual materials that blend well with the surrounding rocky terrain. The deep, wide sand treads provide a nonslip surface and allow space for randomly planted low clumps of alpines.

Trees planted at the boundary along the road ensure a degree of seclusion to the open, sunny garden. They also cast welcome shade on hot summer days.

Grassy areas form a pleasing and relaxing contrast to the "wild" boulder-strewn hillside, which is brightly colored in summer but rugged and lifeless during the winter months.

▲ **Sun and shelter** Carved from the underlying bedrock, a plateau close to the house has been leveled sufficiently to accommodate a sitting area. It appears to emerge naturally from the surrounding rocks and enjoys the summer sun for most of the day.

colder gardens. Such plants include members of the succulent Crassulaceae family: sprawling and mat-forming stonecrops with acid-yellow, rich pink, or white flowers and fleshy or plump foliage; and houseleeks, with their sculptural rosettes and flowers carried on curiously thick and ungainly stems.

Although some rock-dwelling plants prefer light shade, trees and rock gardens are not a happy blend. In autumn the leaf fall can smother and rot delicate plants, and dense shade and drips from overhanging branches are lethal to alpines.

The two horse chestnuts and clipped privet pillars that mark the roadside boundary do not encroach on the sunny, open space

▲ **Drystone walls** Hewn from local stone, the stepped wall echoes the rise in the rocky landscape. Laid dry, the wall provides a home for self-sown seedlings of red valerians and golden alpine wallflowers.

▶ **Rock plants** Porous rock, such as limestone, collects water and organic debris in every tiny crack and fissure. Sedums and houseleeks *(Sempervivum)* colonize readily in the bare minimum of soil, spreading their evergreen leaf rosettes over bare rock surfaces.

that the alpine plants demand. There are few large shrubs, but at the top of the gentle slope an Irish heath stands sentry by the terrace. For a heath *(Erica)* species, it is surprisingly alkaline tolerant. It flowers from Christmas until early summer.

Compact clumps of low-growing evergreen gorse, indigenous to the area, add a wild note and bright yellow spring color to the surrounding rocks.

Color and form
The color scheme is pleasantly relaxed and flexible. It includes bold hues — bright reds, oranges, and yellows; soft hues — pastel mauves and pinks; and white. Both traditional and unexpected color combinations occur in the small clumps of plants, but because the color is diluted by the expanse of rock and lawn none of the colors clash. On a smaller scale, clumps of rock-plant foliage, ranging from mounds of deep green grasslike thrift to succulent gray houseleek rosettes, serve as a soothing backdrop for strongly colored blossoms.

Many of the plants self-seed in unexpected places, and others are allowed to ramble, intermingle, and spread unchecked for a natural effect. Even the stone risers of the steps provide homes for rock garden plants, while native ferns and valerian cling to the drystone walls.

Though some purists might feel that plants should eventually cover every exposed stone surface in a rock garden, the large proportion of rock serves here to reinforce the wildness of the garden and adds a sense of drama.

Late spring is a good time for color in this garden, as it is with many alpine and rock plants growing in the wild. Apart from the tulips, there are clumps of arabis, primroses, aubrieta, aurinia, and wallflowers. However, bright color continues all through the summer, beginning with huge clumps of white-flowered dame's rocket (which will self-seed freely), followed later by deep pink mallows, soapwort, dianthus, aromatic lavender, and thyme.

Self-seeded pot marigolds span three seasons, carrying their cheerful orange flowers from late spring until the first fall frosts arrive. And there are enough evergreen plants to keep the garden from looking excessively bare in winter.

GARDENING BY THE SEA

**Strong winds and salty sprays, together with
bright sunshine and a temperate climate, create conditions
that favor tough but colorful plants.**

On calm summer days, this seaside garden overlooking a picturesque harbor presents an idyllic picture. But gardening by the sea is a constant battle against the elements, a compromise between the forces of nature and human inventiveness. Howling gales and salt- and sand-laden winds can flatten plants and scorch their foliage. Even in the milder parts of the southeastern and Pacific coasts, damage from salt sprays can be severe; thus successful gardening is possible only behind a windbreak.

Wind barriers
The best windbreaks for seaside gardens are hedges or dense groupings of evergreen or deciduous trees and large shrubs. The choice of suitable plants depends on the climate and exposure — on northeastern shores, the plants must be able to withstand not only spray and drought but also frigid winds. There, extra-hardy shrubs such as rugosa roses, bayberry *(Myrica pensylvanica),* or sea buckthorn *(Hippophae rhamnoides)* work well, especially if backed up by hardy trees such as white spruce *(Picea glauca)* and Scotch pine *(Pinus sylvestris).*

On milder southern and western coasts, the choice of wind barriers is wider, including evergreen oak *(Quercus ilex),* tamarisk, and brooms as well as elaeagnus, some cotoneasters, hebes, escallonias, and many pines, junipers, and other conifers.

Planting for summer displays
This garden on a mild, nearly frost-free coast covers 840 sq yd (700 sq m). It slopes down to the house, where it flattens out to form a plateau before sloping down again to the harbor. Since this is a vacation home, the garden has been planned for maximum summer impact. The soil is alkaline and free-draining.

Shelter is provided by large evergreen shrubs, and the strong roots of brooms and sea buckthorn prevent soil erosion from denuding the steep, rocky slopes.

The layout
A wide terrace runs along the front of the house facing the harbor, with easy access into the house. An apple tree serves as a focal point and gives shade in midsummer. A low retaining wall separates the terrace from a lawn leading down to the water. Paths connect the terrace to the harbor and the house to the garden.

Shrubs and perennials, chosen to withstand sea winds, form a windbreak around the garden. Small island beds of perennials — yellow coreopsis, blue campanula, and mauve scabiosa — are planted in the lawn; in summer they become bright, colorful splashes against the green.

▶ **Clifftop view** Overlooking a sheltered little harbor, the view of the lighthouse and the sea beyond is framed by the golden flowers of *Coreopsis verticillata,* russet-red spirea, and pink annual mallows *(Lavatera trimestris).*

Local stone is used for drystone retaining walls, which have been built to link the different levels. They flank either side of the steep steps.

▲ **Wall shelter** Trained against a house wall and framed by Boston ivy *(Parthenocissus tricuspidata)*, climbing roses are less likely to incur wind damage here than in the garden.

▼ **Bird's-eye view** The paved terrace in front of the house, shaded by a mature apple tree, offers a sweeping prospect of the deep inlet and the boats at anchor.

Flagstone paving is used for both terraces and paths, so that one flows smoothly into the other. Instead of fitting tightly together, the large slabs are allowed to "float" in broad mortar beds. The straight edges are softened by foliage and flowers to create a natural effect.

The terrace in front of the house overlooks the harbor. Uncluttered, except for functional furniture, it traps the sun on good days. In inclement weather the stunning view can be enjoyed from behind the French windows.

The furniture, like the house, has plain, simple lines. Both the house and the furniture are painted white to accentuate the color and rich detail of the planting.

Small island beds of vibrant perennials are set in the lawn, making bright splashes of color against a background of green. They are true maritime plants, reveling in the bright light.

N

▲ **Trailing clematis** Rather than face the wind and sea sprays, *Clematis x jackmanii* 'Superba' trails itself into a low mound of purple blooms.

▼ **Seaside stalwarts** Kniphofias, sea thrift, sea hollies, silvery artemisia, and evergreen hebes all flourish in coastal climates.

Fencing between the garden and an old, narrow path along the seaside bluff is hidden by herbaceous perennials and shrubs. These are pruned so that they never interfere with the spectacular view, while still providing privacy. The fencing keeps family pets in and stray animals out.

Plantings

The dense windbreak planting includes elaeagnus, escallonia, and olearia, which provide tough evergreen foliage and flowers. The elaeagnus blossoms are tiny but have a strong scent of vanilla. The bright pink tubular flowers of escallonia and the cheerful daisylike flowers of olearia are at their best in summer.

Equally suitable windbreaks for southern and western coastal gardens would be *Euonymus japonica* or *Griselinia littoralis;* both are evergreen and can be clipped or grown informally.

For the most exposed conditions, sea buckthorn (*Hippophae rhamnoides*), with its silvery willowlike leaves and long-lasting glistening orange berries, is ideal. Sea buckthorn has the additional advantage of strong, deep roots, and it is often planted to stabilize sand dunes. (At least one male plant is needed to ensure good crops of berries on the females.)

Tamarisk is another good windbreak shrub in the South, and has delicate pink-lilac flowers in summer. However, it rarely succeeds in alkaline soil.

Among the ornamental trees are the golden-leaved black locust (*Robinia pseudoacacia* 'Frisia'), cluster pine (*Pinus pinaster*), and silver wattle (*Acacia dealbata*). This last flourishes only on sunny, virtually frost-free sites, where it produces its fluffy yellow flowers in mid- to late winter. Juniper, arbutus, and eucalyptus are other, hardier options.

The tough, spreading roots of senecios and brooms help to retain the soil on the steep slopes. Other shrubby plants are buddleia and various hebes (which flourish by the sea), spireas, and tree mallows (*Lavatera olbia*).

Perennials grown for summer flowers include campanula, feverfew, achillea, anthemis, erigeron, Shasta daisy, daylily, helenium, coreopsis, and scabiosa. Though flag iris *(Iris × germanica)* flowers in early summer, its attractive

spiky leaves add to the summer display.

Red-hot pokers *(Kniphofia)* perk up the garden from midsummer onward, when the first flush of early flowers is over. Annuals include pink-flowered mallow *(Lavatera trimestris)*, sea lavender, and poppies.

Upkeep of the lawn is the major maintenance commitment. More minor chores include deadheading, applying fertilizers and mulches, and planting the occasional replacement shrub.

Color combinations

Color in the garden is bright and cheerful. Warm colors, especially yellow, are featured, and unsophisticated, contrasting color combinations fill beds and borders. For example, purple clematis grows near yellow evening primrose; purple-leaved berberis is next to yellow achillea. Yellow daisies and bright red climbing roses, yellow coreopsis and purple asters, and yellow broom and purple lavender are other partners.

Bright, even startling, color is used, but the effect is never garish — the greenery of wind barriers provides a cooling and unifying setting, within which the patches of color can glow.

▲ **Seaside perennials** Yellow coreopsis and anthemis, pale mauve scabiosas, pink achilleas, and silvery lamb's ears join together to provide plentiful summer color.

Though this is not primarily a foliage garden, ornamental grasses such as miscanthus, as well as ivy, ornamental vines, and ferns, are grown for their attractive leaves. Gray and silver foliage plants — such as lamb's ears, lavender, senecio, artemisia, rue, rosemary, pinks, santolina, and catmint — are the mainstay of seaside gardening.

Seaside adaptation

Many plants have naturally adapted to coastal climates. Lamb's ears *(Stachys byzantina)* are covered with fine hairs as a protection against the wind and salty spray. Most senecios are similarly equipped, and garden pinks *(Dianthus)* have leaves covered with a waxy coating that serves the same purpose.

Other plants dispense with leaves altogether, replacing them with thin green shoots, notably gorse *(Ulex)*, tamarisk, and the Spanish broom *(Spartium junceum)*. Others develop a tough outer layer to the leaves, as in *Euonymus japonica*, the evergreen oak *(Quercus ilex)*, and sea buckthorn *(Hippophae rhamnoides)*.

The intensity of light by the seaside encourages exceptionally vivid colors in such half-hardy annuals as gazanias, mesembryanthemums, and osteospermum.

▶ **Sweet lavender** Tough, gray-leaved, scented lavender lines the cliff path down to the harbor, and strong-rooted shrubs bind the sandy soil.

PLANTS FOR SEASIDE GARDENS				
NAME	**DESCRIPTION**	**HEIGHT**	**SPREAD**	**SITE**
Armeria maritima (thrift)	Evergreen alpine; grassy leaves; pink flower globes in early summer	2-3 in (5-7.5 cm)	6 in (15 cm)	Well-drained soil; sun
Echinops ritro (globe thistle)	Hardy perennial; gray-green thistlelike leaves; blue globelike flowers in summer	3-4 ft (90-120 cm)	2 ft (60 cm)	Well-drained soil; sun
Escallonia rubra hybrids (escallonia)	Evergreen shrub; dark green leaves; pink or red flowers from summer to fall	6-10 ft (1.8-3 m)	6 ft (1.8 m)	Any well-drained soil; sun
Fuchsia hybrids (fuchsia)	Deciduous shrub, bushy or trailing, for mild areas; drooping flowers in a range of colors from summer to fall	2 ft (60 cm)	2 ft (60 cm)	Rich, well-drained soil; sun or light shade
Hebe species (hebe)	Evergreen shrub for mild areas; small gray, green, or golden leaves; white or blue flower spikes from summer to fall	2-60 in (5-150 cm)	6-36 in (15-90 cm)	Well-drained soil; sun
Helianthemum nummularium hybrids (rock rose)	Evergreen shrub; light green leaves; roselike white, yellow, pink, or red flowers in summer	4-6 in (10-15 cm)	2 ft (60 cm)	Well-drained soil; sun
Hippophae rhamnoides (sea buckthorn)	Deciduous spiny shrub; narrow silvery leaves; small yellow flowers in spring; red fall berries if plants of both sexes are grown	8 ft (2.4 m)	8 ft (2.4 m)	Well-drained soil; sun or light shade
Kniphofia hybrids (red-hot poker)	Perennial; grassy leaves; spikes of red, yellow, orange, or cream flowers in summer	2½-3 ft (75-90 cm)	2-3 ft (60-90 cm)	Well-drained soil; sun or shade
Olearia species (daisybush)	Evergreen shrub for mild areas; oval, green, white-felted leaves; daisy flowers in summer	4-8 ft (1.2-2.4 m)	4-8 ft (1.2-2.4 m)	Rich, well-drained soil; sun
Osteospermum species (African daisy)	Perennial for mild areas; lance-shaped downy leaves; yellow, pink, or blue daisy flowers from late spring to late fall	1½-2 ft (45-60 cm)	1 ft (30 cm)	Rich, well-drained soil; full sun
Rosa rugosa (rugosa rose)	Deciduous prickly and suckering rose; wrinkled pale green leaves; pink or white flowers in summer	7 ft (2.1 m)	4 ft (1.2 m)	Deep well-drained soil; sun
Tamarix species (tamarisk)	Deciduous shrub; pale green leaves; pink flower sprays in late spring or late summer	10-15 ft (3-4.5 m)	10 ft (3 m)	Well-drained, lime-free soil; sun

A SHELTERED COASTAL GARDEN

Natural shelterbelts filter the wind from the sea and also create a protected inner zone in which many tender plants will flourish.

Seaside gardens, especially along the southern and western coasts, often enjoy milder climates and a higher degree of light intensity than sheltered inland gardens. However, they are beset with problems, notably those caused by strong sea winds and salty sprays. Exposed sites, which bear the full force of the prevailing, often wet winds, can be turned into spectacular gardens behind ample shelterbelts that protect an inner zone, in which low-growing and tough seaside plants survive and flourish.

Coastal haven
The garden described here is on two distinct levels. The upper part surrounds a level shelf on which the house, facing due south, is situated. The lower part of the garden drops sharply down to the shoreline 60 ft (18 m)

below. The soil is a sandy, free-draining acid loam, which is ideal for rhododendrons and other acid-loving plants. The underlying subsoil is part clay. Frosts are rare, since the prevailing winds are temperate oceanic ones. As a result, the gardeners have been able to cultivate lush vegetation that would not survive a few miles inland.

This garden is spacious, but it has features that could easily be adapted to much smaller coastal or exposed sites.

Originally the upper section had two beech trees and some evergreen oaks that were kept trimmed to hedge height. The lower slopes were a jungle of bramble and blackthorn, with two or three birches and several white willows.

Because of the coastal position, the first task was to provide plen-

ty of shelter, particularly at the more exposed perimeter.

Taming the wind
The first line of defense against the wind was to run tall wooden fences down each side of the garden. Next, for quick all-year protection, the western boundary was planted with evergreen Leyland cypresses. This windbreak has gradually been extended with eucalyptuses, bay trees, rhododendrons, and escallonias, which are particularly good as their sticky leaves shrug off salt.

Two beech trees planted near

▼ **Wind protection** A dense belt of mixed deciduous and evergreen trees and shrubs filters the wind from the water. Mixed borders, banks of heathers, and raised beds of low-growing perennials and alpines lie in its shelter.

◄ **Atlas cedar** A specimen plant of the blue-leaved *Cedrus atlantica* 'Glauca' towers above an underplanting of summer-flowering heathers on the lower slope of the garden. This fast-growing tree needs plenty of space.

the boundaries not only give protection from the wind but also supply some filtered shade for an underplanting of rhododendrons, azaleas, and camellias. The pink camellia flowers make a beautiful spring combination with drifts of white daffodils. Here, too, are hostas and hardy cyclamens (*Cyclamen coum* and *C. hederifolium*) in pink and white forms.

At the foot of the lawn, evergreen oaks (*Quercus ilex*), a handsome tough species with leathery evergreen leaves, were allowed to grow into trees. Hawthorns were planted in this area, behind variegated pittosporums and griselinias — both good evergreens for mild coastal gardens.

The lower slopes were cleared of scrub and planted with groups of trees and shrubs as a shelterbelt. Willows and the original birches, kept low by the wind, were retained in order to filter the wind and reduce its strength before it enters the upper garden.

The informal groups of trees and shrubs are separated by grass walks planted with crocuses and

COASTAL COLOR

In spite of the exposed conditions, the mild seaside climate and sunny site encourage the flowering plants in the mixed border (shown opposite) to provide color for an extended period. A shelterbelt gives some protection from the wind, and tall, floppy plants that need to be staked have been avoided. All of the plants used here are hardy and will perform equally well, or better, in cooler inland gardens. The plan on the right identifies some of the main plants. The border is shown at the beginning of midsummer.

1 Shelterbelt
2 *Spiraea japonica* 'Goldflame'
3 Cottage pink (*Dianthus* 'Mrs. Sinkins')
4 Columbine (*Aquilegia vulgaris*)
5 Rugosa rose (*Rosa* 'Blanc Double de Coubert')
6 Jerusalem sage (*Phlomis fruticosa*)
7 Love-in-a-mist (*Nigella hispanica*)
8 Spurge (*Euphorbia epithymoides*)
9 Perennial wallflower (*Erysimum linifolium*)
10 California poppy (*Eschscholzia californica*)
11 Mountain bluet (*Centaurea montana*)
12 'Pacific Coast' hybrid iris
13 Dutch hybrid iris

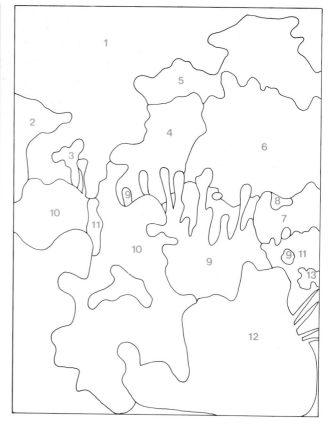

colchicums for early and late color. Mediterranean rock roses *(Cistus)* thrive in the dry soil and the extra warmth that is created by the sun's rays striking the south-facing slope at a right angle.

Flowering borders

A wide mixed border beside the lawn gives a colorful display for much of the year. Trees and shrubs, including eucalyptus, bay, *Prunus subhirtella*, amelanchier, rugosa roses, and mahonias, provide a solid background for the flowers and smaller shrubs in front. Most of the trees and shrubs are fairly tough and easy-going — while the least hardy, such as eucalyptus, are frost shy but tolerate a certain degree of wind.

Bold groups of old-fashioned plants, like *Dianthus* 'Mrs. Sinkins,' columbines, love-in-a-mist, perennial wallflower, mountain bluets, hardy geraniums, and snapdragons, are interplanted among the shrubs.

Here, several African daisies

55

◀ **Terraced beds** Two rock garden beds have been created from excavated soil and contained within walls of natural stone. Alpine plants and low-growing shrubs, including pink-flowered rock roses *(Helianthemum)*, flourish in the bright light and provide a colorful foundation for the adjacent shrubs.

▶ **Maritime associates** The evergreen lantern tree *(Crinodendron hookeranum)* is spectacular in late spring when long-stalked crimson lanterns droop from its branches. Requiring neutral to acid soil and light shade, the lantern tree thrives only in the mildest frost-free regions. It is partnered here by the hardier blue-leaved and graceful cider gum *(Eucalyptus gunnii)* and a glossy-leaved camellia.

▼ **Graceful lines** The curved lines of a deep mixed border and a crescent-shaped heather bank help to break up the wide expanse of lawn. At its far end lies a sunken paved garden, protected from the wind by a shelterbelt of trees.

(Osteospermum) also enjoy the sun at the border's front, and there is contrasting swordlike foliage from *Gladiolus byzantinus* and irises. Because of the wind, tall, floppy plants that require staking have been avoided.

The compact shrubs in the border were selected for their colored foliage: bright *Spiraea japonica* 'Goldflame,' *Weigela florida* 'Variegata,' grayish-leaved Jerusalem sage, hebes, and olearias.

Beyond the long border, the boundary fence is clothed with hardy fire thorn *(Pyracantha),* offering glossy leaves, flowers, and berries. In front of a stepped entrance to the lower slopes,

honeysuckle intertwines with *Clematis montana.* The profuse flowers of both continue over a long season.

Lawn features

A generous expanse of lawn is broken up by the interesting focal points specially created for the exposed site.

Where the lawn dips slightly near the house, a crescent-shaped rock-covered bank is planted with heathers to give year-round color.

There are other ground-hugging plants that are particularly suitable for a windy site. They include thymes; the alkaline-hating, blue-flowered *Lithodora diffusa* 'Grace Ward'; and the prostrate shrub *Leptospermum rupestre* with white flowers and glossy green leaves.

At the end of the lawn there is another small change in level. This is the sunken garden, paved with stone. At the entrance, it is softened by a covering of thyme. The excavated soil was used to form rock gardens on each side of the paving. On the inner sides the soil is retained by low, sloping rock walls; next to the lawn, more rocks help to support the soil. Thyme and thrift, both hardy, drought-tolerant plants, have taken a firm hold in the retaining walls.

Single- and double-flowered rock roses *(Helianthemum)* in many colors, pale blue *Veronica gentianoides*, gray-leaved pinks, and other sun-loving rock plants flourish in the free-draining soil.

Several shrubs add height to the sunken garden: a thorny elaeagnus with gold-splashed leaves *(Elaeagnus pungens* 'Dicksonii'), a buckthorn with silver-edged leaves *(Rhamnus alaternus* 'Variegata'), and other variegated shrubs. These all can be seen from the house standing out against the shelterbelt beyond.

Wall cover
Climbing roses, including the lovely *Rosa banksiae*, which flourishes in hot, sunny sites; a mature wisteria; and a somewhat tender winter-flowering honeysuckle — all enjoy the protection of the house walls.

▲ **Wind filter** Large pollarded willows form sizable windbreaks, as their wide-spreading branches slow down the force of the wind and prevent salt sprays from reaching the ornamental planting in the inner garden.

◀ **Evergreen foliage** Coastal gardens can look desolate in winter, but evergreen shrubs prove effective throughout the year. The golden-leaved shrub *Euonymus fortunei* 'Emerald 'n Gold' is a striking focal point when seen against a dark green deodar cedar (*Cedrus deodara* 'Pendula'), which is kept low and drooping with regular pruning.

A WINDSWEPT GARDEN

An exposed site offers panoramic views, but creating a garden there requires both living and inanimate windbreaks and the use of wind-resistant plants.

A garden on a high, windswept site may suffer from a number of ills. In the North, its plants may die in winter more readily than those in more sheltered neighboring gardens. Exposure to the wind while their roots are frozen and cannot absorb water will cause plants to dehydrate. In the Midwest and Plains states — terrain famous for its unbroken (and unsheltered) sweep — another and equal threat is the arid winds of summer. In the Southwest, of course, a garden open to the wind is soon reduced to a near-desert condition, and in the Southeast, an unprotected garden is vulnerable to a wintry "norther," an arctic wind that sweeps down from the North to freeze and kill unprotected garden plants.

Carefully arranged windbreaks — formal hedges or, better yet, irregular belts of tough trees and shrubs — provide the best solution to such a situation. Pockets of calm form in the lee of such plantings, allowing lush plants to flourish in dry lands and tender plants to bloom in the North. Couple this with a skillful use of plants naturally resistant to wind, and gardeners may have a landscape as verdant as that on the quietest site.

One windproofed garden

The garden pictured here and on the following pages sits high on a coastal plain and is naturally swept by winds through much of the year. It was converted from an old farmyard and has an uninspiring rectangular shape — which the gardener has cleverly disguised by filling the garden with a mixture of curved and straight beds and borders.

The garden is still bordered by the old farmyard walls. The longest of these lies to the south and provides good shelter for perennials and shrubs. Few plants survive above the wall as the wind is a severe trimmer of foliage. Even the low shrubs grow close together for protection. The northern boundary wall is higher; a grapevine and several fruit trees are trained along it.

The house is bordered by a neat pathway made of square quarry tiles, which doubles as a patio in one sunny corner. The straight lines of the path are obscured by the cottage-style planting spilling over from the raised beds. Another path — a curving ribbon of gravel — leads through the garden from the back gate to the northwest corner.

The eastern side of the garden is almost self-contained. A short, curving path divides the fruit and

---

▼ **Eastern exposure** A dense evergreen wind barrier of spindle trees (*Euonymus japonica*), bay laurel (*Laurus nobilis*), and griselinias offers needed protection to the lawn area. Ground-hugging shrubs, alpines, and fall bulbs thrive in the shelter of the windbreak.

▲ **Sun roses** Though punishing at times, warm oceanic breezes make it possible to cultivate frost-sensitive plants such as x *Halimiocistus*, a dwarf evergreen shrub with pure white flowers in summer.

▼ **Alternative lawns** Where foot traffic is light, ground covers offer attractive alternatives to turf. This soft and aromatic "lawn" is actually composed of chamomile.

vegetable section from the main lawn. In turn this lawn is separated by a gravel path from another, smaller lawn planted with sweet-scented low-growing chamomile instead of grass.

The central part of the garden is pleasantly intimate and secluded, being bounded on one side by a high evergreen windbreak hedge and on the other side by a banked shrubbery.

The central area also features a rose bed, flanked by a cobblestone pavement. Planted among the stones are herbs, including thyme and marjoram, and self-sown wild strawberries.

Behind the shrubbery, to the west, is a second cobbled area, which forms a sheltered courtyard. Small areas of cobblestone have been removed here to make informal herb beds, which are planted with perennial species such as thyme and chives and annuals such as basil, parsley, summer savory, and chervil.

Local stone has been used to construct raised beds and rock gardens and to frame lower beds — creating a variety of levels. Raised beds planted within drystone walls follow the L-shaped line of the house, to the west.

Ground-cover plants

By maintaining such a low profile, these plants escape the effects of even the most violent winds. They are a mainstay of this garden, appearing to best advantage in the rock garden that runs parallel to the house wall.

Here are planted the dwarf yellow-flowered St.-John's-wort (*Hypericum × moseranum*), pinks, campanulas, and lady's mantle (*Alchemilla mollis*), while the raised bed is full of brightly colored low shrubs such as the crimson-flowered *Spiraea japonica* 'Anthony Waterer' and rock roses.

Dense mats of knotweed (*Polygonum affine* 'Darjeeling Red') make superb ground cover. This plant sports striking red leaves in fall and winter, long after its deep pink flower spikes have faded.

A sloping bed runs along the other side of the gravel path, partly covered by a blanket of *Clematis × jouiniana,* which in fall has masses of small white flowers, tinted lilac. This bed also contains lavender cotton, white-flowered candytuft (*Iberis*), and hellebores.

▲ **Patio shelter** In the lee of the house, a quarry-tiled sundeck overlooks low raised beds bright with color. Wisteria and roses climb the house walls, and sweet-scented catmint *(Nepeta)* spills over the path.

▶ **Sea thrift** Raised beds in drystone walls provide the well-drained conditions in which coastal plants, such as the pink-flowered sea thrift *(Armeria maritima)*, thrive.

Choosing plants

The nearness of the sea means using salt-tolerant plants for windbreaks, such as the Japanese spindle tree *(Euonymus japonica)*. This is a sturdy evergreen shrub, densely branched and with glossy dark green and leathery salt-tolerant leaves.

Intermingled with the euonymus are other evergreens, notably bay laurel *(Laurus nobilis)*, *Griselinia littoralis* with leathery apple-green rounded leaves, and several tough *Elaeagnus pungens* plants. Late-flowering nerines and early irises grow in the bed protected by the shrubs.

Shrubs by the south wall include dark red-flowered broom, hebes, and *Weigela florida* 'Variegata,' with its pink flowers and

▲ **Drystone walls** The farmyard walls give warmth and shelter to a miniature conifer landscape. A small pool is stocked with *Iris pseudacorus* and edged with prostrate junipers.

▼ **Herb garden** Space has been created in the cobbled courtyard for culinary herbs such as mint, thyme, and lemon balm. Self-sown seedlings of wild strawberry appear among the herbs.

a mass of bright red berries in fall and in winter.

Two skimmias, ideal shrubs for coastal and inner-city areas, mark the entrance to the central part of the garden; they seem to love hostile conditions. Male and female flowers are borne on separate plants, so both are needed for an annual crop of gleaming red berries.

A sturdy specimen crab apple stands in the lawn. This tree bears an abundant mass of white flowers in late spring and an equally plentiful harvest of purple-red fruits, which can be used to make jelly.

Cotoneaster and winter jasmine line the south wall, bordering the lawn. The winter jasmine survives remarkably well; it flowers in late fall, creating an attractive display in combination with the chrysanthemums planted on the field side of the wall.

If sheltered, fuchsias also do well here, blossoming into fall. Hydrangeas, hebes, and the New Zealand daisybush *(Olearia)* enjoy the bright light, combining well with the purple-leaved plant *Phormium tenax* 'Purpureum.'

Lavender and rosemary are good choices for scent and robustness. At ground level, natural seaside plants such as candytuft *(Iberis sempervirens)* and thrift *(Armeria maritima)* bloom in summer, together with garden pinks and creeping blue bellflowers *(Campanula carpatica)*.

cream-edged leaves. The purple-flowered *Daphne odora*, which is excellent for early-spring color and is sweetly scented, grows in a narrow bed below the wall, along with a bright mixture of perennials, including sea hollies *(Eryngium maritimum)*.

More shrubs in the central courtyard area form a protective and decorative edging.

A long row of escallonias backs the shrubbery. These robust shrubs are good seaside plants and are very popular for hedging.

Here, cultivars bear bright rose-red flowers, set among dark green glossy leaves, throughout the summer and well into fall.

In front of the escallonias, hardy berberis and hypericum cluster around gray-leaved senecio, giving some protection to the frost-tender Mexican abelia *(Abelia floribunda)*, which bears tubular cherry-red flowers in early summer. The tough prostrate *Cotoneaster* 'Hybridus Pendulus' flows down the slope of the bank and out over the cobbles, spilling

A SWIMMING POOL GARDEN

**An elegantly simple design turns a swimming pool
into a garden centerpiece, while guaranteeing both low
maintenance and a relaxed poolside ambience.**

A private swimming pool is a luxury that many people dream about, especially during long, hot summers. However, it can easily overwhelm a garden, for to be of any use a swimming pool must occupy considerable space and enjoy a favorable site — the comfort of swimmers dictates a spot open to the sun but sheltered from the wind. On large properties, it may be possible to install a pool at some distance from the house, where it can be wholly or partly screened from the rest of the landscape. However, in an ordinary yard, it is more sensible to incorporate a pool into the overall house and garden picture and to design the garden around the pool.

Before getting caught up in the design process, be sure to check the local ordinances governing pools. Typically, for instance, building codes demand the enclosure of a pool with a wall or fence. You should also temper your plans with reality: consider not only the expense of installing the pool you want, but also the cost of maintaining it. Be sure to get bids from several reputable contractors before committing yourself to any particular design.

▼ **Swimming pool design** Appearing as a natural extension of the house and terrace, the streamlined pool is open to sun and light, with white-painted walls providing shelter and privacy.

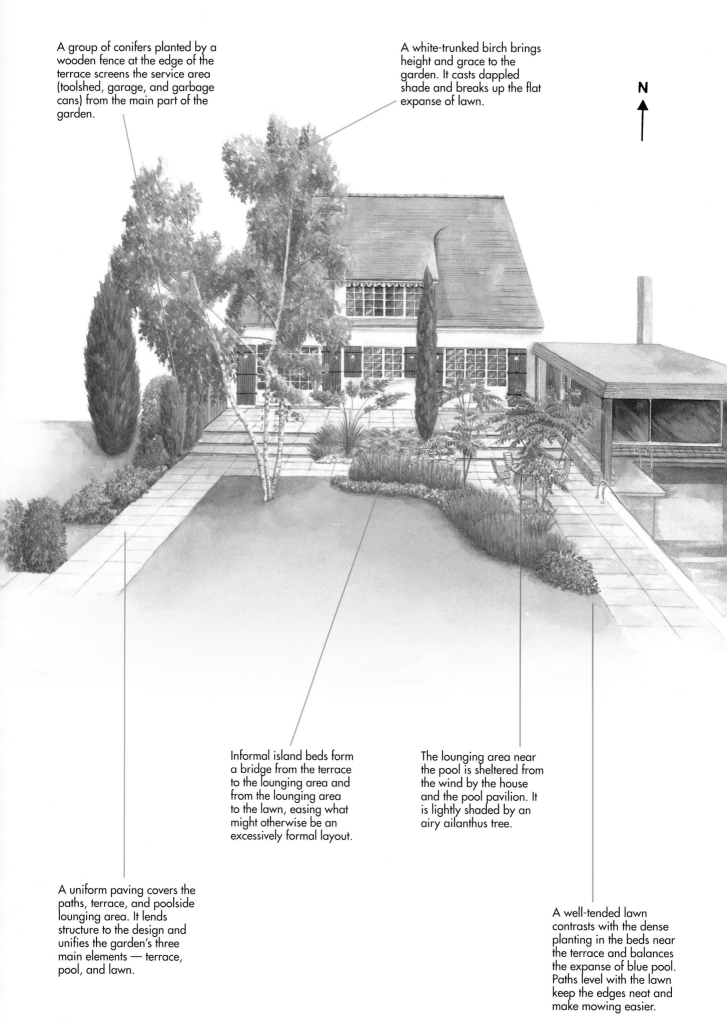

A group of conifers planted by a wooden fence at the edge of the terrace screens the service area (toolshed, garage, and garbage cans) from the main part of the garden.

A white-trunked birch brings height and grace to the garden. It casts dappled shade and breaks up the flat expanse of lawn.

N

Informal island beds form a bridge from the terrace to the lounging area and from the lounging area to the lawn, easing what might otherwise be an excessively formal layout.

The lounging area near the pool is sheltered from the wind by the house and the pool pavilion. It is lightly shaded by an airy ailanthus tree.

A uniform paving covers the paths, terrace, and poolside lounging area. It lends structure to the design and unifies the garden's three main elements — terrace, pool, and lawn.

A well-tended lawn contrasts with the dense planting in the beds near the terrace and balances the expanse of blue pool. Paths level with the lawn keep the edges neat and make mowing easier.

Walls, whitewashed to match the house, provide a measure of safety from accidents, as well as privacy and shelter, and reflect light into the garden.

The pool is the main feature of the garden, but it is positioned so that it does not dominate the scene.

The setting

The house and garden featured here are set on a sheltered suburban lot. The swimming pool and garden have been designed to take full advantage of the sun and to provide a low-maintenance and tranquil green setting, which is ideal for rest and play.

The house is built on a slightly raised part of an almost flat site, which creates a natural platform for a large terrace outside the back door.

The main feature of the garden as a whole is the swimming pool. Such a pool is a major investment, both in money and space, in any garden, and it has been designed for maximum use. The glass-enclosed pavilion beside the house contains changing facilities as well as the pumping, filtering, and heating units. It also provides a sheltered walkway with direct access to the pool.

Structural details

The terrace directly behind the house, combined with the pavilion, pool, and boundary walls, gives a pleasant, neat-looking form to the garden.

The rectangular areas of paving and water are balanced by an even larger area of lawn, whose shape is defined by paths down either side. The paths emphasize the formal shape of the pool and provide a practical edge to the lawn, making mowing far easier and preventing grass clippings from drifting into the water.

The paving extends beyond the end of the pool to give an impression of wide space at the rear of the garden, away from the house. The gentle slope of the lawn adds

▶ **Specimen trees** Planted in the vicinity of the house but well away from the pool, young and mature trees create a light woodland atmosphere and lift the view from the horizontal perspective of the terrace and lawn. They also cast welcome shade on hot, sunny days.

◀ **Ground-cover plants** Carpets of prostrate evergreen cotoneasters smother weeds and provide year-round color while softening the edges of paving and steps. In a low-maintenance garden, such ground covers are easily kept neat with an annual trim. In spring naturalized bulbs add patches of color.

▶ **Poplar screens** Airy trees, such as poplars and birches, add height without the disadvantage of dense shade. Large trees should be kept well away from a pool to avoid the nuisance of leaves in the water and possible damage to the structure of the pool from spreading roots.

▼ **A room with a view** The covered walkway beside the house has glass doors that lead straight to the pool. This structure provides a welcome refuge if the weather turns cold.

to the overall feeling of spaciousness. Steps leading down from the terrace toward the lawn are interrupted by a rectangular island bed that is edged with pebbles to provide contrast with the surrounding sharp-edged paving. Pebbles are particularly appropriate in this situation; close to the water, they create the illusion of a pebbled beach.

The lower part of the terrace opens out to create a generous sitting and eating area in dappled shade, sheltered by the pavilion and surrounded by planting beds. One rectangular bed is set into the shallow steps and another fills a corner of the lawn and provides the only softening of the rectangular lines of the terrace, paths, and pool.

The service areas — a garage, a small toolshed, and a place for the garbage cans — are hidden behind a fence and rows of conifers, which suggest a hedge without forming a solid barrier. The beds between are planted with low-growing cotoneaster for a handsome ground cover.

Planting patterns
Four mature poplars provide a splendid backdrop to the view from the terrace. Tall columnar

trees are ideal in such a site, since they offer height and screening without producing dense shade.

Early-summer color is provided mainly by banks of rhododendrons. Careful choice of shrubs can give year-round interest: the rhododendrons are interspersed with other evergreen and deciduous shrubs, and even in the heart of winter the dark green domes of rhododendrons provide a perfect contrast to the leafless, feathery poplar branches above.

Closer to the house a European birch *(Betula pendula)*, with its delicate arching habit and white trunk, balances the solid rectangular lines of the pool and paving.

A successful feature of this pool garden is the way in which mature trees have been incorporated into the design. All trees should be sited well away from a pool, to prevent leaves from falling into the water in fall and to keep catkins from dumping thousands of seeds in late spring. Many trees also have wide-spreading roots that can fracture house and pool foundations.

The birch is sited in the open lawn in the angle formed by the path and the terrace — a position that shows off its white trunk and delicate shape to perfection for year-round enjoyment.

In the opposite corner of the lawn, close to the pool, a bed of evergreen ground-cover plants, including lavender and heather, is interspersed with small specimen trees, which shelter the sitting area. Among them are tree-of-heaven *(Ailanthus altissima)*, with its attractive ashlike leaves and clusters of red-brown fruits, and several low-growing conifers.

Plants in the island bed between the steps include the strong spiky shapes of a giant dracaena *(Cordyline australis)*, irises, and ornamental grasses. These all contrast with the soft, drooping roundness of the leaf canopy of a staghorn sumac *(Rhus typhina)*. Further contrast and height come in the form of a pencil-slim Italian cypress *(Cupressus sempervirens)*, with low-growing dwarf conifers arching at its feet.

Introducing color
For most of the year the main colors in the garden are the cool, clear blue of water set in rich

67

green surroundings. Late spring brings a burst of color at the end of the garden, where the rhododendrons come into bloom. This is followed by the yellow daisylike flowers of *Doronicum* and the colorful blooms of selected summer bedding plants, massed together to give a good display.

The garden has been designed to look attractive throughout the year. In fall the leaves of many of the trees turn brown, red, or gold, and during the winter months the bare branches of the deciduous trees form a delicate tracery against a background of evergreen color — bold upright conifers contrasting with the gentler domes of the rhododendrons and the green sweep of the prostrate ground cover.

For extra color, pots, tubs, and hanging baskets are introduced on the terrace area and the steps in summer. However, the overall impression is of an elegant and restrained garden, with spare, lean lines and a refreshing green openness that provide a perfect setting for the swimming pool centerpiece.

▼ **Swimming pool design** Formal and free-form pools are equally popular, but for the largest swimming area, the formal or rectangular pool is preferable. Such a pool complements the clean, straight lines of a formal landscape setting.

POOL SENSE

A swimming pool represents a large investment, so look at the project from all angles and give it very careful consideration before going ahead. To many people, pool maintenance is an unnecessary extra chore and expense — don't assume a pool will add to the value of your property.

Pool installation is a specialized type of construction that requires a mastery of the problems involved in creating a watertight structure and knowledge of drainage. For this reason it is best to employ a contractor who specializes in pools. Be sure to request (and check) references from previous customers.

Planning Type, size, and materials all affect the price. To admit the machinery necessary for excavation, an access path at least 6 ft (1.8 m) wide is essential. The most gracefully shaped pools are made by spraying concrete over a wire-mesh base. Liner pools, with a thick sheet of vinyl lining either a metal or a concrete shell, or reinforced concrete are other options.

One popular size is a rectangle 3 x 10 yd (2.7 x 9 m), usually referred to as a lap pool. Rounded corners or a curved, stepped end soften the lines. Also popular are larger rectangular pools and the free-form curvaceous kidney or teardrop shapes. A depth of 5 ft (1.5 m) is adequate for most swimmers, though the pool should be shallower if small children use it. For diving allow a depth of at least 8 ft

(2.4 m). If you intend to include a diving board, check local codes for the required depth.

Site the pool in a sheltered spot close to the house, or you may need to add an extra building to provide changing rooms and to house filtering, pumping, and heating equipment; a pool cover; tools to keep the pool clean; and deck chairs.

A nonslip path or terrace around the pool is a good idea; it gives the structure a neat finish and provides access year-round. Include a nearby sitting area, and use plastic or wooden slatted furniture, which will not be harmed by wet clothes or splashes. Keep plants away from splashing pool water. (This will also keep the water free of plant debris.)

Heating and lighting In cooler climates, heating the pool will greatly extend the swimming season and the swimmer's enjoyment. Choose from electrical, gas, or oil-fired units. Solar power and heat pumps will provide backup heating, but are not sufficient on their own in any but the sunniest regions. An insulated cover helps to keep heat in when the pool is not in use and acts as a safety feature.

Lighting enables you to make greater use of the pool in the evening and casts an attractive glow around the pool area. Underwater lighting is spectacular. As a safety feature, lighting should define the edge of the pool at night.

Shady and damp sites

Shade can be an asset in the garden, rather than a problem. In fact, gardeners often try to create shade where it is missing. A number of plants require some degree of shade, and many others readily adapt to being in the shade for part of the day. Although the density of shade varies from the dark shadows cast by neighboring buildings to the dappled shade from a tree canopy, every garden catches some light, and much can be done to reflect the sun from the surrounding walls and from overhead.

Shady gardens can become cool and refreshing retreats — foliage plants, especially, thrive in moist, shady sites, and leaf variegations are much more pronounced there than in bright sun. Many rose and clematis blossoms fade and do not color properly in areas of intense light. Especially in the South, they may perform best in lightly shaded sites.

Shade and damp soil usually accompany each other, providing wonderful opportunities for growing moisture-loving plants and creating miniature woodland gardens. The banks of streams and ponds are the natural habitat of sculptural gunneras and ornamental rhubarb, as well as ferns, primulas, and marsh marigolds — all plants that are difficult to grow in an open, sunny garden. A problem patch of permanently wet ground can be transformed into a showpiece when it is converted into a bog garden, brightly colored from early spring into fall.

Moist shade Ferns, ivies, primroses, and wood anemones all flourish beneath a leafy canopy.

DAPPLED SHADE

**Sun filtering through trees creates
ever-changing patterns of light and shade among green
foliage and subtly colored flowers.**

Gardeners often regard shade as a problem, but it can be an asset. Many plants flourish only in the shade, and many more are shade tolerant, so a wide range of plants can be grown in a shady garden.

Shade adds a sense of mystery to a garden, with some areas appearing dark and undefined while others are endowed with changing patterns of light and shade as the sun moves across the sky overhead. Most important, shade is tranquil, restful to the eye and to the mind. This peaceful quality can be accentuated with some well-chosen plants.

Shade varies greatly, in degree and in quality, and may be dense, open, or dappled. Dense shade imposes the greatest restrictions, but even here a number of shade-loving shrubs and perennials will thrive (see chart on pages 85-86). Only the most sun-loving plants — such as desert-dwelling cacti — object to partial or dappled shade, though many species flower and fruit less prolifically than in sunny sites and may grow excessively tall.

▼ **Tranquil greenery** The predominant green hue in this shady garden is restful to the eye and offers infinite variations in tones and textures. A dark mound of boxwood contrasts well with a golden-leaved spirea and clumps of silvery lamb's ears.

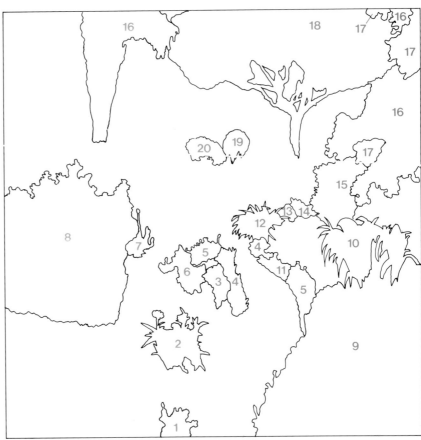

LIGHT AND SHADE

The plan identifies the main plants shown on the left. In this mainly green garden, dim areas contrast with stretches of golden light.

1 Cranesbill (*Geranium macrorrhizum* 'Album')
2 Mountain bluet (*Centaurea montana*)
3 Lady's mantle (*Alchemilla mollis*)
4 Viola hybrid
5 Forget-me-not (*Myosotis sylvatica*)
6 Purple avens (*Geum rivale*)
7 Oriental poppy (*Papaver orientale*)
8 Myrtle (*Myrtus communis*)
9 Dead nettle (*Lamium maculatum* 'Variegatum')
10 Yellow flag (*Iris pseudacorus*)
11 Creeping Jenny (*Lysimachia nummularia* 'Aurea')
12 Spurge (*Euphorbia characias wulfenii*)
13 Fringecup (*Tellima grandiflora*)
14 Cranesbill (*Geranium himalayense*)
15 Hortensia (*Hydrangea macrophylla*)
16 *Laburnum anagyroides*
17 Lilac (*Syringa vulgaris* 'Vestale')
18 Apple
19 Common box (*Buxus sempervirens*)
20 Peony (*Paeonia lactiflora*)

Soil plays an important part in the choice of shade-loving plants. Shade combined with moist soil, such as that found in woodland areas, will support a greater wealth of plant life than shade with dry soil.

Dappled shade

The kind of shade found beneath trees with a lacy overhead pattern suits a range of woody and herbaceous plants. Green is a restful color and forms the backbone of shady gardens, but since there are many nuances of green it is never monotonous. For many golden green plants, shade is es-sential for preventing sun scorch. There are many different colorful flowers that can brighten the greenery, but it is a good idea to avoid strong colors, whose brilliance is lost in dim light, and to settle for subtle, pale colors that become almost luminous in the dark.

The small suburban garden shown here faces north and occupies a 40 ft x 100 ft (12 m x 30 m) lot that is attached to a turn-of-the-century house. Old brick walls form the boundaries and are topped here and there with panels of vertically louvered boards for extra privacy.

▶ **Plants for shade** At ground level, a rich mixture of flowers and foliage includes the pinkish blooms of purple avens *(Geum rivale)*, mountain bluets, and the pink blossoms of variegated dead nettle, which spreads to form an evergreen carpet that is in bloom for most of the year. The buds of Oriental poppy are about to burst, and the pale green palmate leaves of lady's mantle await their decoration of lime-green flower sprays.

▼ **Golden foliage** Useful for brightening dark corners, many yellow-leaved plants prefer dappled shade, where strong sun cannot scorch their thin leaves. Lit by the filtered sun are a golden-leaved currant *(Ribes sanguineum* 'Brocklebankii') and *Spiraea japonica* 'Goldflame.' Climbing the wall is a golden ivy *(Hedera helix* 'Buttercup') and at its feet the arching pale green fronds of the ostrich fern *(Matteuccia struthiopteris)*.

Access from the house is by means of a conservatory. If you look at the house from the back of the garden, the conservatory flowers and foliage add to the effect. The lot slopes away from the house, then levels out to form a roughly circular lawn, surrounded by dense planting for shelter.

The lawn is loosely curved, creating informal asymmetry and generous planting beds. With the dense planting around it, the lawn has the pleasant feeling of an enclosed dell. To one side, a pool is tucked into the planting.

Stone steps from the conservatory down to the lawn are set into the slope. From the lawn, a gently curving flagstone path enters the woodland garden beyond.

Mature lilacs and apple, pear, bay, and laburnum trees add to the sense of peace and seclusion.

Focal points

The small concrete pool is the main ornamental feature. The water attracts a wide range of wildlife, including toads, frogs, and newts, so there's often animal life to observe as well as an array of water plants. Natural stones clustered around the pool create a realistic setting and also provide winter quarters for toads.

In keeping with the period of the house, a cast-iron table is used for poolside meals. Its crisp white form placed against the greenery makes it an effective focal point from the house as well as from the garden.

There is relatively little paved area — a flagstone path and some pale stone slabs placed here and there. The style is very simple, so that nothing competes with the plants for attention.

Shade-loving plants

Shades and tints of green predominate, with tiny sparks or drifts of seasonal color derived from flowers. The proportion of green to other colors is much the same as that in a woodland garden. As in the woodland garden, many different colors appear, with no colors excluded.

▶ **Woodland glade** In spite of the suburban setting, this lot has all the tranquillity of a secluded country garden. The play of light through the trees and tall shrubs creates a marvelous dappled effect. Mature trees are carefully thinned to allow the sun and light through.

Variegated golden- and silver-leaved plants are tightly grouped and surrounded by enough plain greenery to avoid clashes.

The garden contains unusual plants and the occasional plant with dramatic foliage — golden New Zealand flax (*Phormium tenax* 'Aureum') and *Rodgersia aesculifolia*, for example — but relaxed informality is the theme, and nothing stands out as exotic. Most cultivars have the modest appearance of wildflowers, with small blossoms and a natural grace.

Shrub plants include choisya, golden spirea, golden-leaved flowering currant, hortensias, and tall bamboos.

Herbaceous perennials fill the gaps between shrubs. Some are undemanding ground-covering plants such as periwinkle, hostas, golden and spotted dead nettle, lady's mantle, violas, species geraniums, and golden creeping Jenny. Other easygoing perennials include geums, poppies, dicentras, crocosmias, centaureas, fringecups, and various spurges.

Self-seeded biennials and annuals include forget-me-not and sweet alyssum. In spring daffodils and tulips are followed by bluebells. Ivy, golden hops, and *Actinidia deliciosa* clothe the walls.

The pool contains a wealth of water and waterside planting, with marsh marigolds, sweet flag, and water iris in the pool, and moisture-loving alliums, hart's-tongue fern, lady fern, cranesbills, and Solomon's seal on the

▲ **Forest pool** Home to frogs, toads, and newts, a small pool fits naturally into the woodland setting. The pool is too shady for water lilies, but marsh marigolds, globeflowers, and yellow flags thrive here. Solomon's seal, *Saxifraga umbrosa*, hart's-tongue fern, and lady fern grow on the banks.

banks. Even *Saxifraga umbrosa* tumbling over the stones manages to look wild.

The garden is designed so that maintenance is kept to a reasonable level. Organic fertilizers are applied annually.

Readjustments in planting take place occasionally, if one herbaceous species overruns its neighbors or a shrub begins to obstruct a fine view. Trees are thinned to allow light through.

LIGHT SHADE

Enclosed by buildings and high walls, a shaded garden receives enough indirect light for a multitude of plants to grow.

Many town or city gardens are shady, as they are often enclosed by buildings, walls, or tall trees. Yet the shade is rarely dense because the gardens are open to the sky. While they may have little direct sun, they receive indirect and reflected light. Many plants will grow in shade and shelter, and some revel in just such conditions.

You can increase the impression of light in semishaded sites by using pale-colored surface materials that are in keeping with surrounding walls and by combining different paving materials such as concrete and brick. To bring a dull corner to life, use a surface topping of white pebbles or crushed stone.

This small, shady city garden is surrounded on three sides by buildings, with a boundary wall completing the enclosure. It is vulnerable to strong crosswinds and takes a long time to warm up

in the spring. The design is based on constructed landscape features — a pool, raised beds, and paving — combined with imaginative shade-loving plantings.

The site

The garden was originally the flat backyard of an attached row house and covered with rubble. The only feature retained from the former garden is a concrete path. The rest of the site was dug over, the rubble removed to a depth of 2 ft (60 cm), and the soil then enriched with bonemeal and well-rotted manure.

A brick buttress, halfway along the perimeter wall, lends a vertical element to the design. Like a pointing finger, it draws attention to the raised beds and to the pool. An attractive brick pathway connects the original concrete paving to the pool and raised beds.

The raised beds are built on a

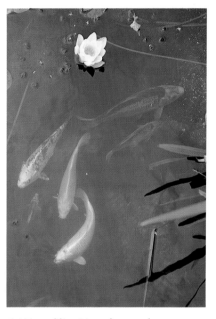

▲ **Water lilies** *Nymphaea odorata sulphurea* is the perfect water lily for a small pool. It keeps its pure yellow color well in suffused light.

▼ **Architectural emphasis** The blue-gray spurge (*Euphorbia characias wulfenii*) is of shrublike proportions and has dense yellow-green flower bracts. Like most other spurges, it grows well in dry, shady soil.

foundation of the rubble removed from elsewhere in the garden. The walls are of brick and mortar and topped with a neat coping of bricks set edgewise. Soil from the excavated pool, well enriched, has been used to fill the raised beds.

The plants

The pool is filled in summer with variegated water grasses and the fragrant water lily *Nymphaea odorata sulphurea*. Hardy, but not too vigorous, with deep sulfur-yellow flowers and mottled red-brown leaves, this water lily is ideal for a small pool. Half a dozen attractively colored koi carp swim beneath.

In the crescent-shaped bed by the edge of the pool grow *Hosta sieboldiana,* with its beautiful blue-green crinkled leaves, and Japanese irises *(Iris kaempferi),* which flower in midsummer.

A variegated periwinkle cascades from the raised bed above; any frost-damaged leaves are trimmed away annually in spring. It is partnered by nasturtium, with its orange-red and yellow flowers; baby's breath *(Gypsophila);* and lavender. Other plants in this bed include a variegated sage *(Salvia officinalis* 'Icterina'), a yellow shrubby potentilla *(Potentilla fruticosa),* and white flowering tobacco *(Nicotiana).*

A small raised alpine bed abuts the other end of the pool. It contains miniature conifers — the upright, conical *Juniperus communis* 'Compressa,' the black spruce *(Picea mariana* 'Nana'), and the dwarf Alberta spruce *(Picea glauca* 'Conica') with bright grass-green needles.

This bed also holds an extensive range of alpine plants, including echeverias, saxifrages, dwarf irises, and angel's-tears narcissi *(Narcissus triandrus).* A deciduous cotoneaster is kept severely trimmed, in order to stop it from swamping the entire bed.

Color schemes

Light-colored shrubs and flowers have been used to brighten the shady site. In summer the colors include whites, creams, yellows, blues, and violets, with splashes of flame and orange.

Pink and white tulips, plus daffodils and narcissi of various colors and shapes, populate the ground-level beds in spring.

▲ **Level changes** Raised beds contained within brick walls add interesting height variations to a flat site. Clematises are planted at the back, with their roots in the cool shade of annuals and clumps of lavender.

▼ **Bold sweeps** A curved bed by the pool introduces a different geometric shape, which is repeated in the nearby curving brick path. Curves and changes in level help to disguise the garden's rectangular lines.

A strong vertical line is provided in the southwest corner by the upright *Robinia pseudoacacia* 'Frisia,' a golden-leaved cultivar of the black locust. This, with the raised beds and tall plants such as *Euphorbia characias wulfenii*, lends a third dimension to an otherwise flat garden.

The small lawn is strictly aligned with the raised beds and pool, but the splash of green has a softening effect in a garden structured mainly with masonry.

N

HOUSE

A brick pathway connects the older concrete paving with the borders, a grouping of raised beds, and a sunken pool. The path curves gracefully around the large poolside bed and fronts a curved border at the foot of the boundary wall.

Raised beds and a pool divide the garden into small, manageable segments and provide a variety of strong shapes. A brick buttress on the boundary wall draws attention to the raised beds and pool and adds a strong vertical element to the design.

The pastel-colored theme continues into mid- and late spring, when double white *Clematis alpina* 'White Moth' tumbles over the boundary wall, its roots shaded by a cover of white violas. In the bed between the wall and the brick path are white *Delphinium* 'Galahad' and the daisylike flowers of feverfew.

Blue and violet flowers provide an interesting shift of color in late spring and early summer. Lungwort *(Pulmonaria)* in the bed by the pool provides a soft mass of pink and purple-blue blossoms from the end of spring onward. Vigorous *Clematis* 'Blue Bird,' a hybrid between *C. alpina* and *C. macropetala*, climbs the red brick boundary wall and produces its violet-blue semidouble flowers later than the white clematis, with repeats even later in the season, followed by silky seed heads.

Interesting foliage plants contribute varied colors, shapes, and forms. The statuesque spurge *Euphorbia characias wulfenii*,

▲ **Spring color** Shade is less dense in spring, and evergreen leaf colors and euphorbia flower bracts give an illusion of light. This is helped by daffodils and narcissi, with shell-pink, lemon, and white trumpets.

with dark blue-gray leaves on its semiwoody stems and broad heads of yellow-green bracts, gleams like a beacon in the southeast corner of the pool bed.

Also here is the smaller evergreen *Euphorbia epithymoides* (syn. *E. polychroma)*, with bright green leaves, turning reddish in fall, and flower heads of bright acid-yellow bracts in late spring.

A range of plants with variegated leaves are used to good effect in the garden. There is a variegated bamboo *(Pleioblastus auricoma)* at the base of the raised bed and, farther along, the variegated evergreen *Pittosporum tenuifolium*, with glossy green leaves, suffused with silver and edged with white.

Green-flowered gladioli, perfumed flowering tobacco *(Nicotiana alata)*, and lime-green lady's mantle *(Alchemilla mollis)* provide a restful background to brighter flower colors.

Good use has also been made of ground-cover plants and the underplanting beneath shrubs. Spring-flowering snake's-head fritillaries *(Fritillaria meleagris)* grow along the wall under small-leaved hebes; the gray leaves of these shrubs make a perfect foil for the white and purple bell-shaped flowers of the fritillaries.

◄ **Lily-flowered tulips** Pink and white tulips are planted where shafts of sun break through. Tall-stemmed and long-waisted elegant cultivars such as 'White Triumphator' and 'China Pink' open their flared goblets in spring.

PLANTS FOR SHADE

**Shady garden sites are ideal for a large
number of shrubs, perennials, and foliage plants that
thrive only when protected from the sun.**

Most gardens have a shady spot or two — either permanently or for part of the day — and many gardeners regard these, quite wrongly, as problem areas. Many plants, especially those with shallow roots, need at least some shade if they are to flourish.

Types of shade
Many plants tolerate shade, at least for some of the time, while others thrive only if permanently shielded from the sun. Under conditions of continual shade, choose plants that are true shade lovers — those that are merely shade tolerant may grow satisfactorily, but will produce fewer and smaller flowers and fruits than in a sunny spot, and many shrubs become lanky in shade unless regularly pruned back.

The character of shade has an enormous range, depending on how it is created — by tall buildings, masonry walls, and fences; large wide-spreading trees and shrubs; or large-leaved herbaceous perennials.

Light shade is created where tall, solid structures surround the garden, as is common in cities. Though little or no direct sun reaches the ground, it is open to the sky and receives indirect and reflected light. Many climbers and wall shrubs do well in these situations, which are often sheltered. Some woodland plants and ground-cover plants also do well.

Dappled shade is cast by the lacy patchwork of small and thin-leaved deciduous trees, providing perfect conditions for woodland plants. The soil underneath these

trees is generally rich in leaf mold and, if sufficiently moist, is ideal for shade-loving shrubs with underplantings of bulbs and herbaceous ground-cover plants. In dry soil the choice of suitable plants is more limited, but ivies, euphorbias, and many others will grow here.

Dense shade is cast by broad-leaved trees, such as beeches, lindens, oaks, and especially maples and sycamores. Their large, dense leaf cover blocks out nearly all of the sunlight, and their shallow

▼ **Dappled shade** Candelabra primroses revel in the moist, damp soil of woodland sites with light overhead shade. The crimson-, pink-, and white-flowered cultivars of *Primula japonica* naturalize themselves under such conditions and spread by self-sown seedlings.

root systems rob the topsoil of moisture and nutrients, creating an inhospitable environment for most plants.

Early bulbs, such as snowdrops *(Galanthus)*, species crocuses, *Cyclamen coum,* and winter aconites *(Eranthis)*, which are themselves quite shallow rooted, will provide welcome spring color beneath the naked trees. Ferns and mosses may also colonize and cover the ground beneath such trees.

Few plants will grow beneath conifers, partly due to the heavy shade, but mainly because the soil is usually too dry. However, ivies and several euphorbias tolerate dry soil and heavy shade.

Water dripping from large overhead foliage often damages soft-leaved plants. In this case, choose *Rubus odoratus*, snowberries *(Symphoricarpos)*, mahonias, or the various pachysandras.

Most accommodating of all is *Aucuba japonica* — from zone 7 southward it will put up with heavy shade together with dry, poor soil and air pollution. Cultivars with yellow leaf variegations add splashes of color among somber greens and enliven the scene from fall right through to spring with red berries.

Shade and soil

For the majority of shade lovers, soil moisture is of the utmost importance. While few, with the exception of several ferns, marsh marigolds *(Caltha palustris),* and Japanese primroses, appreciate a truly damp site, they do need moisture-retentive soil.

Plenty of organic matter, such as garden compost, decomposed manure, or sphagnum peat, should be dug in at planting time. Apply a thick mulch to keep the root area cool and moist, and throughout the growing season, water plentifully. Plants growing against north-facing walls need particular attention — they do not receive much rainwater and need irrigation by other means.

A combination of dappled shade and acid soil suits the needs of evergreens, such as rhododendrons, camellias, kalmias, pernettyas, and pieris, and the deciduous witch hazels *(Hamamelis)*. For alkaline soils in a shady spot, choose hydrangeas instead — to make a display as beautiful as that of rhododendrons. Or try planting honeysuckles (shrubby and climbing types); the green and variegated forms of *Elaeagnus;* as well as the shiny-leaved evergreen cherry laurels *(Prunus laurocerasus)*.

Year-round attraction

To get the most from a shady site, concentrate on plants that both enjoy shade and give a year-round display of interesting foliage. The most successful shade gardens are often those that rely on foliage plants, with the odd flower or fruit for contrast.

The acid-loving rhododendrons are rather dull once their glorious flowers have faded, but the evergreen foliage of camellias and skimmias remains attractive. The shade-loving mahonias have everything — handsome, glossy evergreen leaves, golden fragrant flowers, and purple-blue berries. *Viburnum davidii* has white flowers and blue berries. Gold- and silver-variegated forms of *Euonymus fortunei* and *E. japonica* are delightful. Some, such as 'Emerald 'n Gold,' add bright splashes at ground level, and others like 'Silver Queen' stud a shady wall with flecks of silvery white.

Some yellow-leaved shrubs do extraordinarily well in shade as long as they have soil that is well drained but moisture retentive.

◄ **Cool shade** Light shade and rich, moist soil will allow many herbaceous perennials to flower to perfection. Astilbes, with their white, cream, pink, or crimson flower plumes, thrive in such sites. Hostas, which serve only as foliage plants in heavier shade, will often unfold tall, loose spikes of trumpet flowers where the light, though still indirect, is brighter.

► **Foliage colors** Hostas are ideal foliage plants for shady and woodland sites with moist, fertile soil. Their leaf colors are more intense in shade, where they are unlikely to suffer from sun scorch, especially types with pale leaf variegations, such as *Hosta fortunei* 'Albo-picta' and the silvery white *H. undulata*.

Hostas thrive in the lightly shaded boggy conditions found by the waterside; unfortunately so do their chief enemies, slugs and snails.

▼ **Filtered sunlight** Spring-flowering bulbs, including the small *Anemone blanda*, bring cheerful color to the shady garden. They colonize easily in the dappled sun and shade cast by deciduous trees and shrubs before these have fully developed their leaf canopies. Later, even in deep, moist shade, anemones are succeeded by bluebells.

Sambucus racemosa 'Plumosa Aurea,' whose finely cut leaves glow like gold, does very well.

Many of the most dramatic foliage shrubs are true shade lovers, such as the handsome *Fatsia japonica*, which is best sheltered against a wall.

The evergreen *Garrya elliptica*, with handsome winter catkins, also thrives in dry shade, as do the invasive hypericums.

Fall color Several shade lovers assume bright fall colors, including many barberries *(Berberis)*, cotoneasters, dogwoods *(Cornus)*, and spindle trees *(Euonymus)*. In acid soils, callicarpas, witch hazels, and deciduous azaleas also provide fall color. Few are as spectacular, however, as the Virginia creeper and Boston ivy (both *Parthenocissus* species), whose handsome leaves burn scarlet against the dullest north wall.

Flower colors Several shrubs add color to the shady garden. Pastels are more in keeping with the cool and restful atmosphere. The flowering currants *(Ribes)* come with pink, rose-red, or white drooping flower clusters, and delicate pink is represented by *Daphne × burkwoodii*. Evergreen foliage is brought to life

▲ Bedding plants Impatiens, in pastel and bright colors and often with variegated leaves, do well in shady sites and window boxes on north walls, alongside trailing lobelias.

▼ Versatile ivies In the most inhospitable sites — whether dense or light shade, dry or moist soil — ivies climb, scramble, and root as carpets wherever they touch the ground.

gonias, with white, pink, or red blooms. The blue or white *Lobelia erinus*, brightly colored nasturtiums *(Tropaeolum majus)*, and pansies *(Viola × wittrockiana)* also perform well in shade.

Climbers and carpets
Many climbers add color and interest to the shady garden. The various ivies *(Hedera)* will clamber up walls and fences or scramble on the ground — variegated types, though less brilliant in shade, surpass the common green variety. Winter jasmine, *Clematis montana*, *Hydrangea anomala petiolaris*, honeysuckle, several roses, and ornamental grapevines *(Vitis)* are still other choices for a shady wall.

Ground-cover plants are frequently adapted to shade and are useful for hiding bare ground, suppressing weeds, and keeping the soil cool for other plants. Sweet woodruff, lily of the valley *(Convallaria)*, dead nettles *(Lamium)*, and periwinkles *(Vinca)* spread quickly in moist soil, while the blue-flowered *Campanula poscharskyana* is likely to be a

by the scented white blossoms of Mexican orange blossom *(Choisya ternata)*.

The subshrubby *Euphorbia characias wulfenii* is noteworthy for its lime-green flower bracts. Fuchsias will combine well with foliage plants, such as ferns, against whose fronds the delicate bells show to advantage. And, for a bright splash of yellow, choose *Forsythia suspensa*.

Several herbaceous perennials, with upright or bushy habits, thrive in open or dappled shade — plants like foxgloves *(Digitalis)*, columbines *(Aquilegia)*, daylilies *(Hemerocallis)*, cranesbills *(Geranium)*, peonies, monkshoods *(Aconitum)*, filipendulas, and mertensias.

Most of the small spring bulbs, such as snowdrops and winter aconites, also do well in shade. The taller *Iris foetidissima* is unassuming in flower, but it thrives in even full shade, does not object to dry soil, and comes into its own in fall, when the huge seedpods split open to reveal rows of glistening red berries.

Annuals for beds, containers, and window boxes include the green- or reddish-leaved wax be-

rampant grower. Large-leaved bergenias and the delicate London pride *(Saxifraga umbrosa* or *S. × urbium)* provide attractive evergreen leaf cover.

Woodland settings

Few gardens are large enough to establish a real woodland grove, but you can easily create similar microclimates and set up a miniature woodland glade in the dappled shade cast by silver birches, dogwoods, filberts, and witch hazels. Underplant these trees with some spring bulbs — snowdrops, winter aconites, crocuses, daffodils, narcissi, bluebells, and fritillaries.

In gardens with moist soils, wood anemones *(Anemone nemorosa)*, sweet violets *(Viola odorata)*, and primulas may be followed with a selection of trilliums, astilbes, and Christmas and Lenten roses *(Helleborus)*.

▶ **Woodland ferns** In full shade and moist soil, hardy evergreen ferns like *Asplenium scolopendrium*, the hart's-tongue fern, easily reach a height of 2 ft (60 cm). The cultivar 'Crispum' has fronds with crisped, wavy edges.

SHADE-LOVING PLANTS

NAME	DESCRIPTION	HEIGHT	SPREAD	SITE
Ajuga reptans (bugleweed or ajuga)	Perennial ground-cover plant; whorled blue flowers in summer	4-12 in (10-30 cm)	1½ ft (45 cm)	Dappled shade; moist soil
Anemone nemorosa (wood anemone)	Perennial tuber; white flowers in spring, sometimes blue	6-8 in (15-20 cm)	6 in (15 cm)	Dappled shade; humus-rich, moisture-retentive soil
Aucuba japonica (Japanese laurel)	Evergreen shrub; leathery, dark green leaves; red berries from fall	6-10 ft (1.8-3 m)	5 ft (1.5 m)	Light or deep shade; any soil
Bergenia species (bergenia)	Evergreen perennials; glossy, leathery leaves; white, pink, or red flowers in spring	1 ft (30 cm)	10-12 in (25-30 cm)	Dappled shade; any soil, including alkaline
Brunnera macrophylla (brunnera)	Perennial ground cover; heart-shaped leaves; forget-me-not-like flowers in late spring	1 ft (30 cm)	1½ ft (45 cm)	Dappled shade; well-drained but moisture-retentive soil
Buxus sempervirens 'Suffruticosa' (boxwood)	Dwarf evergreen shrub for edging and clipping to shape; glossy dark green leaves	1-2 ft (30-60 cm)	1 ft (30 cm)	Light shade; any soil
Camellia species (camellia)	Evergreen shrubs; glossy leaves; white, pink, or red flowers in spring	6-15 ft (1.8-4.5 m)	4-6 ft (1.2-1.8 m)	Light or dappled shade; moist soil, acid to neutral
Convallaria majalis (lily of the valley)	Spreading rhizome; pairs of linear leaves; white, bell-shaped flowers in late spring	8 in (20 cm)	1 ft (30 cm)	Dappled or deep shade; humus-rich, moist soil
Cornus species (dogwood)	Deciduous shrubs, some with colored stems; white or yellow flowers in spring	10 ft (3 m)	10 ft (3 m)	Light or dappled shade; moist soil
Digitalis purpurea (foxglove)	Biennial or perennial; tall flower spikes mainly in shades of pink, mauve, or white in summer	3-5 ft (90-150 cm)	1½ ft (45 cm)	Dappled shade; any moisture-retentive soil
Elaeagnus species (elaeagnus)	Evergreen shrubs; leathery, glossy leaves, variegated gold or yellow in cultivars	8 ft (2.4 m)	8 ft (2.4 m)	Light shade; any soil including poor and sandy ones
Erythronium dens-canis (dog's-tooth violet)	Corm; maroon-marbled leaves; pink to purple flowers in late spring	6 in (15 cm)	6 in (15 cm)	Dappled to deep shade; moist, humus-rich soil
Euonymus fortunei, E. japonica (spindle tree)	Evergreen shrubs; oval, glossy leaves, often variegated	Up to 10 ft (3 m)	4-6 ft (1.2-1.8 m)	Light shade; wall shelter; any soil

SHADE-LOVING PLANTS

NAME	DESCRIPTION	HEIGHT	SPREAD	SITE
Galium odoratum (sweet woodruff)	Perennial ground-cover plant; white scented flowers in early summer	6 in (15 cm)	1½ ft (45 cm)	Dappled shade; moist soil
Garrya elliptica (silk tassel bush)	Evergreen shrub; gray-green leathery leaves; male gray-green catkins in winter	8 ft (2.4 m)	10 ft (3 m)	Light shade; any well-drained to dry soil; some shelter
Geranium endressii (cranesbill)	Ground cover; deeply lobed leaves; pink flowers throughout summer	1 ft (30 cm)	1½ ft (45 cm)	Dappled shade; any well-drained soil
Hamamelis mollis (witch hazel)	Deciduous shrub or small tree; gold or yellow scented flowers in winter or early spring	8 ft (2.4 m)	8 ft (2.4 m)	Dappled shade; moist, acid to neutral soil
Hedera helix (English ivy)	Evergreen climber; glossy leaves, dark green or variegated gold or silver	50 ft (15 m)	–	Light to deep shade; any soil
Helleborus species (hellebore)	Evergreen perennials; leathery leaves; pink, white, and green flowers in late winter/spring	1½-2 ft (45-60 cm)	1½ ft (45 cm)	Dappled or light shade; deep, moist soil
Hemerocallis hybrids (daylily)	Perennials; arching leaves; lilylike flowers in many shades in summer	2½-3 ft (75-90 cm)	1½ ft (45 cm)	Light or dappled shade; any soil
Hosta species (plantain lily)	Herbaceous perennials; pleated leaves, attractively marked or edged	2 ft (60 cm)	1½ ft (45 cm)	Light or dappled shade; humus-rich, moisture-retentive soil
Hydrangea species (hydrangea)	Deciduous shrubs and climbers; light green leaves; white, red, or blue flowers	6 ft (1.8 m)	6 ft (1.8 m)	Light or dappled shade; loamy, moisture-retentive soil; shelter
Hypericum calycinum (aaronsbeard)	Ground cover, spreading shrub, may be invasive; golden flowers in summer	1 ft (30 cm)	Indefinite	Light or dappled shade; well-drained to dry soil
Ilex species (holly)	Evergreen shrubs; spiny green or variegated leaves; red or yellow berries in winter	18 ft (5.4 m)	10 ft (3 m)	Light shade; any soil, best in moist loam
Iris foetidissima (stinking iris)	Evergreen, rhizomatous perennial; purple flowers in summer; orange berries in fall	20 in (50 cm)	1½ ft (45 cm)	Deep shade; any soil, including dry
Jasminum nudiflorum (winter jasmine)	Deciduous wall shrub; lax stems; golden flowers in winter or early spring	10 ft (3 m)	–	Light shade; any well-drained soil
Lamium species (dead nettle)	Ground covers; rough leaves; white, pink, or yellow flowers in late spring to summer	½-1 ft (15-30 cm)	2 ft (60 cm)	Light to deep shade; any soil, least invasive in poor soil
Lonicera species (honeysuckle)	Mainly deciduous climbers; scented yellow to red flowers in summer	20 ft (6 m)	–	Light shade; any rich and well-drained soil
Lysimachia nummularia (creeping Jenny)	Evergreen ground cover; rounded bright green leaves; yellow flowers in summer	Prostrate	1½ ft (45 cm)	Dappled shade; moist or dry soil
Mahonia aquifolium (Oregon grape)	Evergreen shrub; glossy foliage; golden flowers in late spring; purple berries in fall	5 ft (1.5 m)	5 ft (1.5 m)	Light or dappled shade; ordinary to rich, moist soil
Meconopsis betonicifolia	Perennial; oblong leaves; sky-blue flowers in summer	4 ft (1.2 m)	1 ft (30 cm)	Dappled shade; rich soil, moist but never waterlogged
Pachysandra terminalis (pachysandra)	Evergreen ground cover; rounded, green leaves; white-purple flowers in spring	1 ft (30 cm)	1 ft (30 cm)	Dappled to deep shade; humus-rich, moist soil
Parthenocissus species (Boston ivy, Virginia creeper)	Deciduous, vigorous climbers; dark green leaves, rich fall foliage colors	30 ft (9 m)	–	Light shade; deep, loamy soil; keep moist in summer
Pieris formosa (pieris)	Evergreen shrub; red young leaves; drooping white flowers in spring	6-8 ft (1.8-2.4 m)	10 ft (3 m)	Dappled shade; humus-rich, acid and moist soil; shelter
Polygonatum x hybridum (Solomon's seal)	Perennial; long, stem-clasping leaves; white flowers in summer	2 ft (60 cm)	1½ ft (45 cm)	Light or dappled shade; any well-drained soil
Primula species (primrose)	Perennials; crinkled leaves; flowers in all shades in spring	Variable	Variable	Light shade; moist to wet soil
Symphoricarpos albus (snowberry)	Deciduous shrub; small summer flowers; glistening white berries in fall	6 ft (1.8 m)	8 ft (2.4 m)	Light or dappled shade; any well-drained soil
Tiarella cordifolia (foamflower)	Evergreen ground cover; maplelike leaves; white flowers in early summer	½-1 ft (15-30 cm)	1 ft (30 cm)	Dappled shade; moist, humus-rich and acid soil
Trillium grandiflorum (trillium, wake-robin)	Perennial woodland plant; clump forming; white flowers from spring onward	1 ft (30 cm)	1 ft (30 cm)	Dappled shade; humus-rich, moist soil
Vinca species (periwinkle)	Evergreen, sprawling shrubs; green or variegated leaves; blue or white flowers in spring to summer	4-6 in (10-15 cm)	4 ft (1.2 m)	Light or dappled shade; any well-drained soil

A STREAMSIDE GARDEN

**The banks of natural streams are the perfect
habitat for a lush planting of moisture lovers, whose
deep roots help hold the soil in place.**

A garden with a natural stream or pond can prove to be either a problem or a blessing. There are many attractive aspects to waterside gardening — it encourages rich and varied wildlife, and the sound and movement of water introduce a special tranquillity, which is enhanced by the mirrored reflection of plants and sky.

Natural water is a problem if low-lying banks tend to be flooded in fall and winter and to dry out in summer. Waterside gardening then becomes a near impossibility unless the levels of the banks can be raised, either by terracing or by diverting some of the water at flood time with drains.

Always provide access for the gardener to plantings on streamside banks by firmly embedding flat stepping stones or logs in the banks.

In the small garden described here, flooding is rarely a problem as the narrow stream along the far boundary is bordered by steep banks. The garden itself is divided into two areas: a regularly shaped, average-size front yard and a 70 ft (21 m) wide but shallow backyard with a stream running alongside it. The backyard, from the house to the boundary stream, is only 15 ft (4.5 m) deep.

Although the back of the house faces southwest and gets plenty of afternoon sun, the house is situated in a hollow in hilly country and is subject to cold blasts of easterly winds, especially in the winter. Pockets of cool air take a while to disperse, except during the summer months.

The original topsoil of heavy clay was broken up and replaced with loads of loam that was augmented with liberal amounts of

---

▼ **Golden locust** Close to the bank, the finely divided foliage of a golden-leaved locust *(Robinia pseudoacacia* 'Frisia') casts dappled shade onto the lawn as it slopes down to the stream and the far bank of lush foliage.

well-rotted manure and garden compost. Organic fertilizers and mulches are applied annually to build up a deep, rich soil layer.

The back garden

The garden in the backyard is dominated by a beautifully maintained lawn that runs along the full width of the rear plot and over the near bank of the steep-sided stream, down to the water's edge. To achieve a lawn of this quality requires special care and attention. The bluegrass turf is cut regularly, so that no more than a third of the leaf blades are removed at any one time, and it is always cut to the proper height: 2 in (5 cm) in spring and fall but higher — to a height of 3 in (7.5 cm) — in midsummer. In early fall the lawn is fed with a fertilizer rich in slow-release organic nitrogen, and later in fall or in spring, the turf is aerated with a power-coring machine and top-dressed with compost. The vigorous turf that this care has created is naturally resistant to weeds and diseases — the use of herbicides and pesticides is avoided here for fear that the chemicals might leach into the stream.

A small patio, with access through French windows, is made up of stonelike precast paving blocks. It catches the afternoon sun and is sited to provide a view of the whole sweep of the bank, all the way to the overhanging laburnum at the garden's far corner. On one side of the patio is a large shrub bed, which includes hydrangeas and roses; the house walls are clothed with Virginia creeper *(Parthenocissus quinque-folia)* and clematis. At the other end of the patio, a wood pergola, covered with climbing roses and *Clematis montana*, frames an urn filled with summer annuals.

The stream area

This garden is in the enviable position of having a stream at the bottom of the lot, providing a natural border between it and an adjacent field. The stream is the dominating feature of the garden and has dictated the border planting at its edges.

Along the top of the near bank, on either side of a central archway, two apple trees have been planted in the lawn. Their informal shape and habit contrast with the larger and more exotic-looking golden-leaved locust *(Robinia pseudoacacia* 'Frisia') with its layered, feathery shape and light green leaves. This in turn stands out against the deep green of the lawn.

▼ **Sunny patio** The small sheltered patio offers views of the entire backyard, to the stream and the lush planting on its banks and across the landscape of rolling fields.

A wedge-shaped corner has been turned into a sitting area. The floor is constructed of stone paving, and color is provided by container plants, hanging baskets, and climbing roses. A trimmed fire thorn *(Pyracantha)* and climbing roses on the house wall provide a permanent background for annuals and bedding plants.

An unheated greenhouse is used for raising bedding plants and as winter quarters for frost-sensitive plants.

The golden-leaved locust is an ideal shade tree for a small garden. It is a focal point in the garden, with the trunk supporting climbing sweet peas and the base planted with colorful annuals.

The small patio catches the afternoon sun. Although secluded and shut off from the main garden, it is a good vantage point from which to view the back garden, the stream, and the surrounding countryside.

A wooden pergola does not lead anywhere but breaks the monotony of a foliage-covered garden wall. It is clothed with *Clematis montana* and climbing pillar roses.

A wooden bridge crosses the stream in one corner. The bridge provides access to the planting on the stream's far bank and gives the impression that the garden extends into the adjacent field.

A narrow stream runs along the rear boundary of the garden. The near bank is grassed over, while the far side is thickly stocked with a mixture of shrubs and perennials, most of which are moisture-loving plants or true aquatics. This dense vegetation needs to be thinned out and pruned annually. A beech hedge planted behind the border shelters the far bank.

A bamboo archway frames the view of the opposite bank. Looking through the archway from the house side and seeing just part of the field, framed by vegetation, eases the transition from a domesticated to a wilder landscape. Steps lead down to the stream.

A velvety smooth lawn has been achieved through hard work and regular attention. It is fed and mowed conscientiously, aerated regularly, and protected from wear with stones set flush with the surface where the foot traffic is heavy.

The light-colored leaves of the locust match the foliage of a rounded golden privet bush located in the back border. The trunk of the locust provides support for climbing sweet peas; a small, neat circular bed at its base is planted with lobelias and impatiens.

An informal archway made from sturdy bamboo poles is placed centrally on the bank and provides a framed view of the sweeping fields beyond the garden. Two clematises (the large white-flowered *Clematis* 'Miss Bateman' and *C. alpina*, which has elegantly nodding small blue flowers) and climbing rose cultivars scramble over it.

Three steps leading down to the stream are set into the bank below the arch. There is a mass of vegetation on the opposite bank, which needs regular attention — planting, thinning, and pruning back straggly growth in the fall and then again in spring, when the stream must be cleared of debris washed in by the seasonal rains.

The far boundary

The narrow stream separates the great mass of shrubbery and flowers growing on the stream's far bank from the clean sweep of the lawn on the house side.

The far bank consists of a rich alluvial loam. It is sheltered on the field side by a beech hedge and is planted along its streamside face with a great variety of both foliage and flowering plants

▲ **Field view** A bamboo archway covered with clematis, roses, and perennial sweet peas frames the view of the stream and the arable fields. The far bank brims with astilbes, lady's mantles, lilies, and ferns. On the near side, pansies and petunias provide low ground cover.

◄ **For show only** Erected as a kind of trompe l'oeil, the wooden bridge makes the garden seem larger than it is by suggesting (falsely) that the garden extends beyond the stream's far bank. The bridge's rustic charm is enhanced by a profusion of pink geraniums, blue campanulas, and spreading dead nettles — all flourishing in the moist conditions.

◀ **Stepping stones** The immaculate green lawn is unmarked by hard wear. Stepping stones, laid just below the grass level to aid mowing, form an unobtrusive path that links the different parts of the garden.

▼ **Streamside planting** The far bank is lush with moisture-loving foliage and flowering plants, in spite of rigorous thinning out every year. Different leaf colors and shapes show up vividly against pink lilies and astilbes, blue bellflowers, and lime-green alchemillas. The purple foliage of a smoke tree *(Cotinus coggygria)* lends dramatic contrast.

that thrive in the moist conditions. Near the bridge straddling the stream in one corner, a clump of small pink-flowered geraniums grows alongside blue campanulas, ferns, euphorbias, and lamiums, while a perennial sweet pea trails onto the bridge.

Farther along the bank are colonies of monkey flowers *(Mimulus* 'Queen's Prize'). These wetland plants thrive in the boggy conditions alongside the stream and produce their yellow and purple-blotched flowers in summer. Yellow loosestrife *(Lysimachia punctata)* adds more color. This moisture-loving plant looks ungainly in a border liable to drying out, but here conditions are perfect and it quickly asserts its expansive nature.

A purple-leaved smoke tree *(Cotinus coggygria)* grows side by side with ferns and pink-plumed astilbes. A couple of hollies give year-round foliage, and a weeping pussy willow provides welcome color in spring. In late summer, the silver-leaved, purple-spiked buddleias are in flower; they attract a variety of butterflies.

The bank is also planted with crocus, daffodil, and tulip bulbs for early-spring color. Later on, in late spring and early summer, other plants come into bloom. These include water irises, such as yellow flag *(Iris pseudacorus)*, and *Iris laevigata* with its deep

royal blue flowers. In late spring spreading clumps of golden marsh marigolds *(Caltha palustris)* appear. These are planted at the base of the bank, with the irises in the streambed.

Awkward corners

A wedge-shaped space in one corner, between the garage and the house, has been turned into an attractive sitting area defined by interlocking precast mock-stone pavers that match those on the patio.

A large wooden seat beneath the kitchen window is flanked by climbing roses and a trimmed fire thorn *(Pyracantha)*, clothed in fall and winter with large clusters of yellow berries. Pots, boxes, and hanging baskets are filled with bedding plants raised in the greenhouse, including lobelias, impatiens, petunias, pelargoniums, mallows *(Lavatera),* as well as bushy and trailing fuchsias. A large urn holds a gray-leaved *Helichrysum petiolatum,* trained, unusually, as a treelike standard; it is not cold hardy here and is overwintered in the greenhouse.

A large bed at the base of the garage wall is planted with a mixture of bedding plants, shrubs, and climbers that provide form, cover, and color all year. The effect of the red brick is softened with the green and variegated leaves of shrubby hollies.

A wrought-iron gate set within a brick arch leads to the outside world and is guarded by a silk tassel bush *(Garrya elliptica).* This quick-growing evergreen shrub is almost weighed down in spring with long, drooping clusters of gray-green catkins. The boundary wall also supports climbing roses, including the scented coral-pink 'Summer Wine,' and the violet-blue *Clematis* 'Daniel Deronda.' English ivy *(Hedera helix* 'Goldheart') partners the annual yellow-flowered canary-bird vine *(Tropaeolum peregrinum)* and, most spectacular of all, a yellow clematis *(Clematis orientalis).*

This vigorous clematis has also been trained to grow from the end of the garage wall over a rustic pole arbor that frames the short path to the greenhouse.

▲ **Island beds** The centerpiece of the front yard is a vivid island bed planted with standard roses and tall trailing fuchsias. The underplanting of summer annuals includes petunias, pansies, and silvery senecios.

The front garden

A wide graveled path leads to the front of the house, against which grow an espalier-trained Morello cherry and a sheet of dark green ivy. Curving beds line the smooth lawn and are planted with golden conifers, shrubby magnolias, herbaceous perennials, and evergreen ground covers.

The focal point in the front garden is an oblong island bed, which in summer is a mass of bright bedding plants, a colorful carpet for standard-trained fuchsias that spend the winters in the greenhouse. When fall ravages these warm-weather flowers, they are replaced with spring-flowering bulbs and an interplanting of dwarf wallflowers and fall- and winter-blooming pansies, which continue to give color for many months.

POOLSIDE PLANTS

Streamside banks and pool borders provide a chance to create striking combinations of moisture-loving plants with dramatic foliage.

The attraction of formal garden pools lies in the classic simplicity of straight lines, a large expanse of water decorated with water lilies, darting goldfish, and perhaps a clump of irises in one corner. The surrounding area should also be kept strictly formal — unadorned paving slabs with a seat or sundial. Informal pools and natural ponds, however, look most effective surrounded by clumps of luxuriant foliage and flowers. But it isn't enough just to grow any selection of moisture-loving plants. Consideration must be given to the overall shape of the grouping as well as to the texture, color, and form of the individual plants.

A flat expanse of water, even in a small pool supporting just a few water lilies, can look monotonous. So it falls to the plants around the water's edge to provide height — tall plants such as irises, grasses, sedges, imposing rodgersias, and feathery astilbes, which, with their erect foliage or flowering stems, lead the eye upward from the horizontal plane of the water.

Tall, erect plants with long, narrow leaves are greatly enhanced if they are grown beside species with large round, oval, or heart-shaped leaves. The bold rounded leaves of golden ray *(Ligularia dentata)* or the umbrella plant *(Peltiphyllum peltatum)*, for example, make a good background for the finely cut leaves of astilbes or the fine stems of a grass or sedge. Hostas are another possibility, with their stylish clumps of broad leaves.

Such ornamental foliage plants are the essence of every poolside planting, but it pays to introduce a splash of flower color.

In early spring a touch of sun-

shine can be brought to the edges of a pool by interplanting the golden marsh marigold *(Caltha palustris)* with western skunk cabbage *(Lysichiton americanum)*, a plant with waxy yellow flowers held 1 ft (30 cm) above the ground. The little carmine-rose *Primula rosea* could be planted in between.

An attractive combination for

late spring and early summer would be a few clumps of yellow flag *(Iris pseudacorus* 'Variegata') in front of *Ranunculus aconitifolius* 'Flore Pleno,' a tall white double-flowered buttercup.

For the summer, create a brilliant partnership by underplanting blue *Iris kaempferi* with informal-looking yellow monkey flowers *(Mimulus luteus)*.

▶ **Foliage contrasts** A luxuriant jungle of dark green foliage is lit by the pale variegations of Siberian bugloss *(Brunnera macrophylla)*, top left, and the cream-striped *Iris pseudacorus* 'Variegata.' Some flashes of color come from yellow-flowered Asiatic primulas and blue-flowered low *Edraianthus* (foreground).

▲ Flowering marginals The attention-grabbing red flowers in the foreground of this scene belong to an astilbe. Available in many species and cultivars (notably the x *arendsii* strain of hybrids), astilbes typically offer neat clumps of finely cut foliage and airy, graceful plumes of flowers ranging in color from this bright red to bold or pastel pinks, peach, rose, cream, and white. Half-hidden by the astilbe's red here are yellow blossoms of monkey flower *(Mimulus)*. This plant has a more sprawling growth habit, which helps to soften the edge of the pool, and its contrasting flower color throws the astilbe's red into relief. On the far side of the water, true calla lilies *(Zantedeschia aethiopica)*, easily recognized by their white flowers and glossy arrow-shaped leaves, bring a cool air of distinction.

◄ Water irises Flowers and foliage are equal partners in this fine midsummer group. The slender, dark green ribbed leaves and porcelain-blue flowers of stately *Iris kaempferi* are accompanied by the more modest monkey flower *(Mimulus lewisii)*, which has pale green hairy leaves and rose-pink snapdragon-like flowers. A pool edging of creeping Jenny *(Lysimachia nummularia* 'Aurea') forms a golden rim beneath the taller plants.

► Marshy plants The water arum or wild calla lily *(Calla palustris)* is a hardy (to zone 2), vigorous plant suitable for the marshy soil between a pool or stream edge and dry land. Its thick, fleshy rhizomes spread to form clumps of glossy heart-shaped leaves, from which rise the distinctive arumlike white flowers that bloom in early summer. Complementing this are the blue-green heart-shaped leaves of *Hosta* 'Frances Williams.' Contrast comes from a clump of cream- and green-striped sweet flag *(Acorus calamus* 'Variegatus'), standing like an exclamation point between them.

▶ **Angel's fishing rod** Also known as wandflower and, botanically, as *Dierama pulcherrimum,* this moisture-loving perennial looks superb as it arches its long, slender stems gracefully over the water, which reflects its purple-red funnel-shaped flowers. Such elegance needs little accompaniment; here it rises from a simple underplanting of gray-leaved *Aurinia saxatilis,* creeping red-flowered thyme, and ground-hugging rock roses *(Helianthemum).*

▼ **Sea of calm** Clumps of *Hosta crispula* bring the foreground alive in this scene with their pleated white-edged leaves. Hostas, in their innumerable cultivars, offer foliage colors from blue to gold. They adapt to a wide range of conditions, from full sun to deep shade, but generally perform best in a moist, humus-rich soil such as this. Backing them up here are the lime-green flowers of lady's mantle *(Alchemilla mollis),* whose floral sprays mask the division between water and land.

▲ **Giant cowslips** Growing to at least 3 ft (90 cm) tall, giant cowslips *(Primula florindae)* thrive in boggy soil and in early summer produce stout stems topped with clear sulfur-yellow flower clusters. They show up beautifully against the bold purplish leaves of *Ligularia dentata* 'Desdemona.' This tall perennial, about 4 ft (1.2 m) high and wide, has striking orange-yellow flowers, which appear when the cowslips are past their best, thus lengthening the season of this partnership.

▶ **Japanese irises** The midsummer blooms of *Iris kaempferi* — up to 8 in (20 cm) wide — must rate as the most spectacular of all marginal plants. Growing here in shallow water, the iris partners the 3 ft (90 cm) tall, pink-flowered *Astilbe* x *arendsii* 'Bressingham Beauty' and, at the back, the horse-chestnut-leaved *Rodgersia aesculifolia.* This has bronze foliage, crowned by plumes of white, pink-tinged flowers on stems up to 6 ft (1.8 m) high — a magnificent background for any planting of tall wetland natives.

COPING WITH BOGGY SOIL

Permanently moist or wet soil provides an opportunity for creating a bog garden and growing attractive moisture-loving plants.

Damp bog soil occurs naturally in low-lying areas near rivers, lakes, and marshes, and in gardens by the sides of ponds and streams. Far from being a problem site, permanently moist soil is the perfect habitat for wetland natives that gardeners commonly call "bog plants." These demand rich, moist soil that never dries out, even in the hottest of summers, and light shade or full sun to suit individual needs.

Natural bog gardens
Unlike true aquatics, bog plants will not thrive in standing water, which rots their roots. Instead, they flourish in soft, spongy soil that is rich in organic matter. If you have a natural stream or pond in your garden, the moist soil alongside it is ideal for bog plants.

To prepare such a site for planting, begin by clearing away all weeds and other unwanted plants. Fork over the soil and put in access paths as needed — path foundations are unnecessary unless you want a very formal, rigid surface.

Improve heavy soils for bog plants by digging in plenty of sphagnum peat, leaf mold, well-rotted manure, or garden compost. If the natural soil is a heavy clay, break it up by digging in coarse sand as well.

Spring and fall are the best times for planting. Make sure that the soil does not dry out around the roots until plants are established. Even though the subsoil may be wet, surface soil can dry out during hot or windy weather — before the new plants have grown over the whole area, shading the soil and reducing evaporation. Apply a mulch of shredded bark to reduce water loss and keep the roots cool.

If slugs become a problem, protect plants by scattering slug bait regularly — in a moist site, these pests can devour entire plants. If you prefer not to use chemicals, set out inverted flower pots among the plants as traps — slugs hide inside the pots during the day and can be removed and destroyed.

Artificial bog gardens
If you want to grow bog plants but don't have a naturally moist site, you can create suitable conditions artificially. The main requirement is to stop soil drainage. Building a bog garden is much like constructing a fish pond, except that you fill the reservoir

---

▼ **Natural bog garden** The banks along a natural stream are ideal sites for moisture-loving plants. The soft, damp, and richly organic soil suits bog plants such as astilbes, with their red and pink flower plumes, and the giant cowslips (*Primula florindae*).

with wet soil rather than with water.

You can build a bog garden as an extension to a water garden — often the most natural-looking setting in a small garden — or as a self-contained unit in almost any other spot. However, for the best results, the site should be more or less level and sheltered from drying winds and full sun.

Self-contained bog gardens are easy to create, but require more aftercare than those alongside a pool. Excavate a cavity of any size 1-1½ ft (30-45 cm) deep in any desired shape — irregular and rounded shapes look most natural. Line the cavity with polyethylene, PVC, or butyl rubber sheeting — as the liner need not be 100 percent waterproof, the sheeting need not be one continuous piece. Tuck the sheeting underneath any existing edging, such as the lawn; or fold it over the surrounding soil and keep the liner firmly in place with bricks or pieces of paving stone. With a

▶ **Banks of green** Moist streamside banks in dappled shade are inhabited by lush clumps of ferns and hostas, with early-summer color from golden globeflowers and blue forget-me-nots. Rhododendrons thrive in the same moist and shady situations.

pointed stick, punch holes at 6 in (15 cm) intervals through the upper half of the liner around the sides, to allow excess water to seep away through the surrounding soil. Do not puncture the base of the liner where drainage must be impeded, so that the soil remains permanently moist. For ease of access to the plants, lay an edging of paving stones around the excavation.

Next, cover the liner with a 4 in (10 cm) drainage layer of gravel, coarse grit, or rubble, and lay upturned pieces of sod or a sheet of burlap on top. This prevents soil from washing into the drainage material. Then fill the cavity with good-quality topsoil enriched

◀ **Eye-catching foliage** Grown for its arresting bronze-green leaves, which resemble those of a horse chestnut, *Rodgersia aesculifolia*, a hardy perennial, can reach a height of 6 ft (1.8 m) in rich, moist soil and light shade. Hostas make excellent companion plants, and primulas add color.

with loam, leaf mold, or well-rotted garden compost. Use a hose to saturate the soil thoroughly until puddles form on the surface; let it drain before leveling any sunken areas.

Plant the bog plants, working from the sides, and avoid trampling the soil, which should remain open and porous. Keep it moist but not waterlogged at all times, watering well during dry spells.

Pool extensions can be constructed in two ways — as a central part of the main pool design, created at the time of the pool's installation, or built at a later date as an afterthought.

To build a bog garden pocket at the side of a new concrete or plastic-lined pool at the time of its installation, see *Self-watering pool pocket* at right. Bog gardens added to the pool later are less successful since it is generally impossible to create a constant seepage of water from the pool into the bog garden without piercing the pool's watertight membrane. Piercing the membrane will cause the pool to drain, killing any fish and aquatic plants inside it.

The only practical means of watering an add-on bog garden is to flood the adjacent pool regularly, allowing water to flow over its edge until a total of 3 in (7.5 cm) or so of water has washed into the artificial bog. For this to work, the bog garden must stand slightly lower than the pool, but it is easy to make a couple of spillways around the lip of the pool to direct the overflow water.

Planting bog plants

Naturally moist soil tends to be associated with semishaded or shaded sites, where direct sun doesn't dry out the soil surface. For this reason, most bog plants prefer some shade.

Unlike a water garden, where falling leaves soon dirty the water, bog gardens can be sited safely under a tree canopy. Any cool spot in the garden will also do.

Irregular drifts of plants look

▶ **Formal bog garden** A moisture-retaining pocket has been constructed alongside a pool to accommodate creeping Jenny, bergenias, London pride, and other bog plants. A slightly raised wood deck makes an ideal walkway from which to tend the plants.

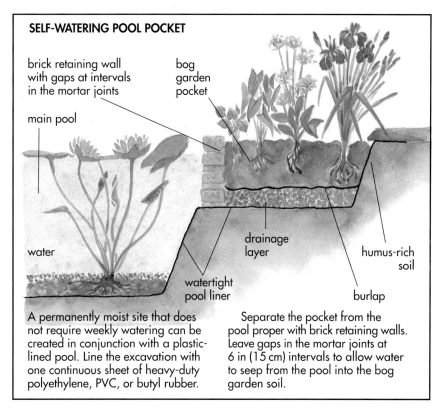

SELF-WATERING POOL POCKET

brick retaining wall with gaps at intervals in the mortar joints

bog garden pocket

main pool

drainage layer

humus-rich soil

water

watertight pool liner

burlap

A permanently moist site that does not require weekly watering can be created in conjunction with a plastic-lined pool. Line the excavation with one continuous sheet of heavy-duty polyethylene, PVC, or butyl rubber.

Separate the pocket from the pool proper with brick retaining walls. Leave gaps in the mortar joints at 6 in (15 cm) intervals to allow water to seep from the pool into the bog garden soil.

more natural than orderly rows or blocks. In general, bog plants are small to medium in size with a height of 1-3 ft (30-90 cm), though there are shorter and taller types. They are best grown in broad and low-lying informal glades, where it is not necessary to gradate the plant heights.

Some bog plants tolerate drier soils in an ordinary border. There is no clear-cut distinction between a bog plant and a border plant. Whether a bog plant needs any special cultivation depends

largely on local soil type, rainfall level, humidity, and the degree of shelter from drying winds.

Permanently wet soil is unpleasant and often dangerous to walk on. Be sure there are plenty of dry paths or stepping stones through and around a bog garden — avoid using very smooth materials, such as slate, as they become slippery when moistened with surface-draining water. Rough-textured concrete or stone paving slabs are among the safest materials for bog garden paving.

BOG GARDEN IN A TUB

A large tub or half barrel can be used to create a miniature bog garden for a patio or other limited space. To ensure that the plants' roots stay cool and that soil moisture doesn't evaporate quickly, you may sink the container below ground to half its depth. Line and fill the tub as for an ordinary bog garden.

▲ **Majestic gunnera** With enormous leaves up to 6 ft (1.8 m) or more wide, the perennial *Gunnera manicata* needs lots of room to spread in a bog garden or at a pool border. The flower cones appear with the young leaves in spring.

BOG AND MOISTURE-LOVING PLANTS

NAME	DESCRIPTION	HEIGHT	SPREAD	SITE
Filipendula ulmaria (queen-of-the-meadow)	Hardy perennial; lobed, toothed leaves; fluffy cream flower heads in summer	3 ft (90 cm)	1½ ft (45 cm)	Partial shade
Fritillaria meleagris (snake's-head fritillary)	Bulb; narrow blue-green leaves; white and purple bell-shaped flowers in spring	1 ft (30 cm)	4-6 in (10-15 cm)	Light shade or sun
Ligularia dentata 'Desdemona' (golden ray)	Hardy perennial; heart-shaped purple-flushed leaves; orange-red flowers in summer	3 ft (90 cm)	2 ft (60 cm)	Light shade or sun
Lobelia siphilitica (great blue lobelia)	Hardy perennial; light green lance-shaped leaves; blue flower spikes in late summer	3 ft (90 cm)	1 ft (30 cm)	Light shade or sun
Phormium tenax (New Zealand flax)	Evergreen foliage plant; swordlike leaves, often variegated	up to 12 ft (3.6 m)	4 ft (1.2 m)	Sun or light shade
Polygonum bistorta 'Superbum' (snakeweed)	Clump-forming perennial; light green leaves; pink flower spikes from summer into fall	3 ft (90 cm)	2 ft (60 cm)	Light shade
Ranunculus acris 'Flore Pleno' (buttercup)	Hardy perennial; deeply cut leaves; bright yellow double flowers in late spring to early summer	3½ ft (105 cm)	1½ ft (45 cm)	Sun or light shade
Thalictrum delavayi 'Hewitt's Double' (meadow rue)	Hardy perennial; light green lacy leaves; sprays of mauve flowers in summer	5 ft (1.5 m)	2 ft (60 cm)	Sun or light shade
Trollius x cultorum (globeflower)	Hardy perennial; lobed finely cut leaves; yellow flowers in late spring to early summer	3 ft (90 cm)	1½ ft (45 cm)	Sun or light shade
Veratrum nigrum (false hellebore)	Hardy perennial; fanlike pleated leaves; maroon flower spikes in summer	5 ft (1.5 m)	2 ft (60 cm)	Light shade

GROWING BOG PLANTS

**A wide choice of moisture-loving plants
and border perennials, both large and small,
flourish in damp and shady conditions.**

In the wild, bog plants grow in damp soil along the sides of lakes, rivers, or streams or on low-lying ground that is regularly flooded or barely above the water table. These are distinguished from truly aquatic plants, which grow with their crowns in shallow water or even totally submerged.

Several plants, such as Japanese anemones, daylilies, monkshoods, and perennial coneflowers, enjoy normal garden conditions and also flourish in moist soil. But best of all, choose plants that *must* have plenty of moisture.

Flowering perennials range enormously in color and form. For spring flowers, choose *Peltiphyllum peltatum* with its soft pink, upright, drumsticklike flowers; *Trollius* cultivars with golden globeflowers; pink-flowered lady's-smock or cuckoo flower *(Cardamine pratensis)*; or bold pink or white bergenias.

Primulas play a major role in the bog garden. The candelabra types, with tiered spikes of showy flowers, are invaluable — they include the red-purple, crimson, pink, or white *Primula japonica* cultivars as well as the pink, orange-scarlet, or salmon hybrids of *P. pulverulenta*.

Drumstick primulas, such as *P. denticulata* with mauve-pink or white flowers, and the Sikkimensis primulas, such as the yellow giant cowslip *(P. florindae)*, offer additional interest in the spring and summer bog garden.

For summer flowers, choose the scarlet-flowered *Lobelia cardinalis* or one of the purple-flowered hybrid lobelias; equally valuable are the pink *Mimulus lewisii* and the scarlet monkey flower *(M. cardinalis)*.

Goatsbeard *(Aruncus dioicus)* adds height to the summer bog garden with its feathery plumes of creamy flowers standing up to 7 ft (2.1 m) tall. In limited space, choose the dwarf cultivar 'Kneiffii.' For similar feathery flowers but a wider color range, opt for ferny-leaved astilbes.

Foliage perennials can be effective in the bog garden, notably ornamental rhubarb *(Rheum palmatum)*, hostas, and *Gunnera manicata*.

Rodgersias have large and handsome rounded or handlike leaves in shades of bronze or green and also produce frothy sprays of cream or pink flowers.

Many ferns thrive in moist soils, and their foliage adds textural qualities to any planting scheme. *Matteuccia pensylvanica* and *Osmunda regalis* are ideal.

Bulbs and rhizomatous-rooted perennials for the bog garden include *Iris kaempferi* and *I. laevigata*, both with mauve, purple, or white flowers, and the white water arum, *Calla palustris*.

Shrubs are usually unsuitable, but shrubby willows with their narrow gray-green leaves and spring catkins are exceptions.

◀ **Destructive beauty** Its pretty purple spikes have made the European loosestrife *(Lythrum salicatia)* a popular import — but American gardeners should shun this plant, which escapes into wetlands to crowd out natives.

▶ **Foliage perennials** A distinguished foliage plant for moisture-retentive soil, *Rodgersia podophylla* has large, ground-covering horse-chestnut-like leaves. They are bronze when young, then green; when fully grown, they develop fine coppery tints. In summer they are topped by tall buff-colored flower spikes. The graceful fresh green fronds of lady fern *(Athyrium filix-femina)*, set against a moss-covered boulder, make a delicate lacy contrast to the bold outlines of the rodgersia.

◀ **Large-scale bog gardens** Many moisture-loving plants have magnificent flowers and foliage, lending themselves to imposing and long-lasting garden pictures.

In this large-scale combination the American elder *(Sambucus canadensis* 'Maxima') is in full bloom in mid- to late summer, its dense 1 ft (30 cm) wide flower heads and large divided leaves forming a strong backdrop for three bold plants. The heart-shaped foliage and deep yellow flowers of *Ligularia dentata* 'Desdemona' make a splash of brilliant color between the glossy paddle-shaped leaves of western skunk cabbage *(Lysichiton americanum)* and, to the right, the enormous rhubarblike leaves of *Gunnera manicata*. After the flowers have faded, the elder puts on a fine display of black berries. It should be pruned hard every spring to keep it within bounds.

▲ **Calla lilies** The gleaming white calla lilies *(Zantedeschia aethiopica)* thrive in boggy soils of frost-free regions, unfolding their glossy spear-shaped leaves and distinctive waxy white flower spathes in spring and early summer.

Here, the callas grow against a magnificent backdrop of *Gunnera manicata.* This impressive foliage plant needs plenty of space to show off its architectural qualities to full advantage. Each leaf, crinkled, lobed, and bristly underneath, may grow up to 6 ft (1.8 m) or more wide and is carried on a prickly stem of much the same length.

◀ **Waterside meadow** An area of damp soil has been densely planted with colorful moisture-loving perennials. The flowers of *Iris sibirica* hover like blue and white butterflies over graceful grassy foliage. *Primula japonica* holds its whorls of pastel-colored and dark-hued blooms like flowering candelabra, surrounded by a sea of yellow monkey flowers *(Mimulus).*

103

▲ **Woodland garden** In an open glade in early summer, robust candelabra primulas thrive in the damp soil. The path of rounds cut from logs looks perfectly at home — though care must be taken when traversing its mossy surface. On the left is *Primula pulverulenta* with whorls of wine-red flowers on white mealy stems about 2 ft (60 cm) tall. Across the way, a carpet of flame-colored *Primula* hybrids burns right up to the base of a matching Kurume azalea.

◄ **Golden buttercups** Globeflowers (*Trollius x cultorum*) are closely related to buttercups and look like larger editions of them. With their rounded golden blooms in late spring and early summer, growing on 2½ ft (75 cm) stems, they make a colorful feature in damp soil, where they will slowly spread.

The pale green, yellow-edged foliage and small whitish flowers of dogwood (*Cornus alba* 'Spaethii') provide a soothing background; gentle contrast comes from the bulbous English irises (*Iris xiphioides*), which are about to open their large flowers.

Gardening on acid soil

Far from being a problem, acid soil supports some of our most beautiful plants and is far easier to manage than thin alkaline soil. Depending on the climate, gardeners using acid soil have their choice of glorious rhododendrons, massive camellias, and summer-flowering heathers. However, a highly acidic soil does not suit all plants, especially roses, vegetables, and most fruits. Fortunately, excess acidity is easily corrected with annual applications of lime to bring the soil closer to neutral — in this respect, a too-acid soil is far easier to correct than one that is excessively alkaline.

Acid soils become difficult when they are also sandy and quick to drain. These soils become too dry and also lack nutrients. Such soils must be enriched with organic materials and annual mulching, and their fertility must be maintained with regular fertilization throughout the growing season.

The exuberant acid lovers — rhododendrons, azaleas, camellias, and pieris — are the glories of the spring garden, but there are plenty of other shrubs and perennials to provide color and interest for the rest of the year. Stunning Japanese maples, bright-flowered brooms, and magnificent magnolias all favor slightly acidic soil, while roses are happier here than on shallow alkaline sites. Exotic lilies, monkshoods, fall crocuses, gentians, violets, and winter-flowering witch hazel are among the many other acid-loving plants.

Acid-loving camellias Magnificent camellias, such as this *Camellia japonica* cultivar, thrive in acid soil.

A GARDEN FOR ACID LOVERS

**Thriving plants can be as clear an indication
of soil type as a soil-testing kit. Rhododendrons
especially flourish only in acid soil.**

Soil acidity and alkalinity are measured against what is called the pH scale. Neutral soils have a pH of 7; readings below that register acid soils and above 7 alkaline soils. The majority of plants flourish in neutral soils; some suffer if the soil becomes too acid, others fail to perform well if conditions are too alkaline, and still others will grow only in markedly acid soils, notably heathers and rhododendrons, which require soil with a pH value of 4.5-6.

Soil testing
You can buy inexpensive, easy-to-use soil-testing kits to establish a soil's acidity and the type of plants it will support. A color-coded chart that's included will show the soil's approximate acidity. You can assess what action you need to take from the readings. Lime is used to bring an acid soil closer to the neutral point; it is much more difficult to turn an alkaline soil into an acid one.

It is also a good idea to take a close look at neighboring gardens; the kinds of plants that flourish there will likely do well in your garden. It is always advisable to choose plants to suit a particular soil type rather than waste time and money on short-term changes to the soil.

Fertility of acid soils
Acid rain generally has little effect on the garden, except in areas of high rainfall or where the soil is very sandy and drains quickly. However, an acid soil may naturally become increasingly acidic, as rainwater leaches out certain chemical nutrients — nitrogen, phosphorus, potassium, sulfur, and calcium. Such acidity can further reduce soil fertility by inhibiting the activity of bacteria and other soil microorganisms — slowing the breakdown of the organic materials, such as fallen leaves, that are the soil's natural fertilizer and pH buffer.

For this reason, it is important to monitor the pH of an acid soil and to add lime if the pH drops below 5. A strongly acid soil may also benefit from the addition of some pH-neutral organic source of humus such as well-rotted manure or garden compost.

Gardening in acid soil
Some of the most popular garden plants, including rhododendrons and azaleas, prefer a loose, quick-draining soil with a high organic content and a low pH.

The garden described here has just such conditions. Although it is at its most spectacular in the

▼ **Acid-soil garden** Spectacular in spring, evergreen hybrid azaleas in dazzling shades of pink are tempered by a magnificent flowering dogwood. In time, the stockade fence will be hidden by a newly planted hedge of mixed conifers and hollies, which will provide shelter and dappled shade for the azaleas.

◄ **Flowering dogwood** The rose-pink *Cornus florida* 'Rubra' is especially appealing near white-flowered azaleas. Its leaves begin to appear as flowering ends and take on rich orange and scarlet tints in fall.

spring, it contains other acid-loving plants that provide vivid color and interest all year. The flat and rectangular garden belongs to a suburban house surrounded by mature trees.

In summer the climate is warm and dry, but winters are cold, with extended periods of snow and freezing temperatures. The formal, geometric layout divides the garden into areas of interlocking paving, lawn, and beds, with a generous flagstone patio. The lawn is bordered by low raised beds built up behind dry-stone walls.

Focal points

The floral centerpiece of the garden in springtime is a large white-flowered dogwood *(Cornus florida)*. Dogwoods range from creeping ground covers to huge forest trees, and though some grow naturally in alkaline soil, this species and the spring-flowering *C. nuttallii* prefer acid soil.

The dogwood flowers themselves are small and insignificant, but in *Cornus florida* and *C. nuttallii* they are surrounded by showy white, pink, or red bracts. There are many cultivars, including weeping forms and some with red-tinged or variegated leaves.

To contrast with the delicate white of the dogwood in spring, the raised beds along the yard's perimeter are filled with clusters of brilliantly colored pink and rosy red evergreen azaleas.

The raised bed by the patio also contains late-flowering dwarf rhododendrons, which provide color once the azaleas are finished. *Pachysandra terminalis* is used as a low-growing ground cover. This plant has perhaps been overplanted in American suburbs, but its tolerance for dense shade or sun, its quick-spreading growth, and its freedom from pests and diseases make it the most practical evergreen ground cover for the northern regions of the country (to zone 5).

Maintenance

This garden is easy to care for. Regular chores during the growing season include mowing and edging the lawn and watering

beds and borders in order to maintain soil moisture. During prolonged dry spells, the azalea and rhododendron foliage is sprayed with water in the evening. Ground cover largely eliminates the need for weeding, and a thick mulch of bark helps to preserve moisture around plant roots, while suppressing weeds at the same time.

Regular pruning is unnecessary, but deadheading helps keep the rhododendrons growing vigorously. The faded flowers should be pinched — not snipped — so no damage is done to the new leaf buds, which sprout immediately below the flowers.

Plants for acid soil

This garden has been photographed in spring, when the display of dogwoods, azaleas, and bulbs is at its best. However, no garden should rely on just one

▼ **Evergreen azaleas** Low-growing azaleas, more delicate in appearance than rhododendrons, show up well in raised beds. Here, their large clusters of bell-shaped flowers and pale green foliage can be better appreciated than at ground level.

▲ **Cool white** The blaze of rose-red azaleas in full bloom could easily be overwhelming, but the almost-white trumpets of clumps of narcissi have a calming effect. The gray color of natural stone walls is also soothing.

▶ **Overhead shade** In late spring, the wide patio is a perfect oasis beneath dogwood flowers of the purest white. Later, the leafy canopy casts welcome shade on hot summer days before turning red, orange, and scarlet in fall.

season's display — gardens need flower and foliage interest for at least some of the rest of the year. Though acid soil is often regarded as difficult to work with, there is no problem in finding a range of plants that thrive in it (see chart on page 140).

Specimen trees

Most dogwoods are hardy, but the young growth of some species, such as *Cornus florida*, is vulnerable to late-spring frosts at the northern end of their ranges. In areas with cool, damp, short summers, flowering dogwoods tend to bloom poorly and are relatively short-lived. Such a climate may also affect the dogwoods' fall foliage, keeping the trees from coloring properly. In these conditions, growing them against a south-facing wall can improve their performance, but a better compact flowering tree for such a site would be a redbud *(Cercis canadensis)*, a serviceberry *(Amelanchier)*, or a crab apple *(Malus)*.

Hawthorns are another good choice of compact flowering trees

for a small garden with acid soil, though their thorns make them unsuitable for households with children. The Washington hawthorn *(Crataegus phaenopyrum)* and the green hawthorn *(C. viridis)* offer the best combination of flowers, fruit, healthy foliage, and attractive form.

An exquisite, long-term option for an acid-soil specimen tree is one of the Japanese maples, such as cultivars of *Acer japonicum* or *A. palmatum*. They make graceful multistemmed trees but take many years to mature and require shelter from strong winds.

Shrubs for acid soil

Most members of the Ericaceae family thrive in acid soil, but exposure to wind and sun and the soil's porosity are also important

factors. For a sheltered, semi-shaded spot, the following shrubs are perfect. *Pieris* species and cultivars provide evergreen cover, colorful spring foliage, and dangling racemes of waxy, white lily-of-the-valley-type blossoms in spring. The spring growth is vulnerable to late frosts and needs shelter from drying winds. *Pieris* shrubs grow slowly, but this is an advantage in a small garden, where fast-growing plants soon outgrow the available space.

Leucothoe fontanesiana also has drooping racemes of white bell-shaped flowers and evergreen foliage, but its growth habit is arching and fountainlike; its leaves turn a rich bronze-purple in fall. It is particularly effective planted at the base of a wall.

The mountain laurel *(Kalmia latifolia)* has clusters of saucer-shaped pink flowers in spring or early summer. White- and red-flowered cultivars are available. Its evergreen leaves are poisonous, so it is unsuitable for planting anywhere livestock is kept.

Bearberry *(Arctostaphylos uva-*

ursi) or wintergreen *(Gaultheria)*, as well as pachysandra, could be grown as ground cover. The first two are evergreen with broad leathery leaves, small clusters of bell-shaped flowers in late spring and summer, and brilliant red fall berries. Ivy, the most tolerant ground cover of all, makes an admirable all-season cover for a planting of winter- and spring-flowering bulbs.

Bulbs and perennials

Many bulbs tolerate a wide range of soils, if the soil is well drained. Some examples include snowdrops and winter aconites in winter; bluebells, erythroniums, fritillaries, and wood anemones in spring; tiger lilies and summer snowflakes in summer; autumn colchicums and snowflakes in fall; and many crocuses from fall to spring.

Most perennials are not fussy as to soil type, but a few will grow only in acid soil. They include the fall gentian *(Gentiana sino-ornata)* and the Himalayan blue poppy *(Meconopsis betonicifolia)*.

▼ **Wisteria in waiting** At the far end of the sunny patio, a wooden pergola painted white will one day be smothered by the trailing stems and drooping, pale mauve flower clusters of a wisteria planted at its base.

A GARDEN OF HEATHERS

**Heathers planted in acid or neutral soil will
bloom throughout the year, spreading vast carpets of
colorful leaves and flowers over the ground.**

Heathers are marvelously versatile. Their long-lasting blooms produce swaths of bright and pastel colors for most of the year. The evergreen foliage is decorative, too, ranging from pale green, gray, and golden to glowing red, russet, and bronze, especially effective in winter. Heathers make an excellent dense ground cover, and as a bonus, many cultivars are good for cutting for fresh or dried flower arrangements.

The name "heathers" is loosely applied to *Calluna* species — small shrubs native to sandy uplands and bogs, most famously in Scotland — and *Erica* species, although the latter are more correctly called heaths. *Calluna* species prefer acid soil, but many ericas, notably the winter-flowering types, flourish in neutral or slightly alkaline soil, and some, like the Mediterranean *Erica terminalis*, prefer alkaline soil.

A heather garden
Although not many heathers thrive in areas of alkaline soil, the owner of the yard pictured here has managed to make do. His garden lies in a coastal area with underlying deposits of alkaline chalk. However, the soil that has accumulated on the surface, blown in or washed in over thousands of years, has a pH just slightly above neutral. By digging in liberal amounts of peat and using acidic mulches such as pine needles, he has created a garden environment in which heathers can flourish.

The irregularly shaped lot is about a third of an acre in size. Sloping gently northeast, the garden receives sun for most of the day. Because of the ocean's moderating influence, summers here are temperate and winters, though windy, are mild.

Winds are the major problem, and a shelterbelt of pines, spruces, and other conifers, many with colored foliage, has been planted around the garden's perimeter.

▼ **Heather associates** In late summer, the heather beds are in full bloom, displaying flower spikes and foliage in a range of both pale and vivid colors. Conifers thrive in much the same soil conditions, and dwarf types stand out like exclamation points above the heather's floral carpet.

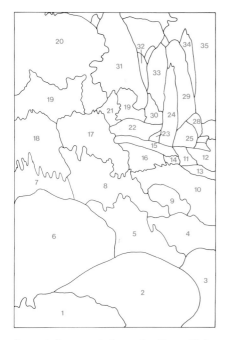

Apart from giving shelter, this evergreen belt provides a good backdrop for the heathers.

Other shrubs, such as variegated hollies, viburnums, *Philadelphus coronarius* 'Aureus,' and *Sambucus racemosa* 'Plumosa Aurea,' are sited in front of the conifers to ease the transition from low ground-cover plants to tall trees.

The garden is approached by a gravel drive, lined on one side by a row of chamaecyparises in various shades of green. On the other side is a mixed shrub border, which includes the male evergreen *Garrya elliptica*, whose long gray-green tassels are so decorative during the winter; hebes; and hardy fuchsias, such as *Fuchsia magellanica* 'Variegata.'

The mixed planting theme continues into the garden itself, where immediately inside the gate is a rare *Piptanthus nepalensis*, an evergreen shrub of the pea family with bright yellow laburnum-like flowers in late spring.

The shrub and tree planting also includes skimmias; *Viburnum tinus* 'Eve Price,' with pink-tinged white flowers in early spring; *Eucalyptus perriniana*, notable for its brown-and-white bark and leaves with a silvery sheen; the fountain dracaena

▶ **Vertical contrast** The spiky fountain dracaena (*Cordyline australis*), though not truly hardy here, survives most winters to emerge dramatically amid mounds of white, pink, russet, and golden heathers.

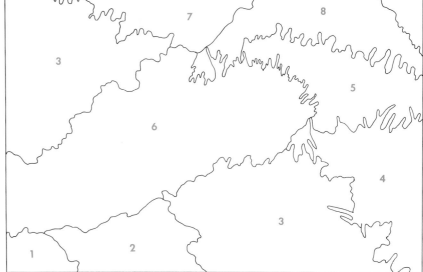

GROUND-COVER COLOR

A weed-suppressing cover (shown above and identified at right) continues to provide foliage interest once flowers are over.

1 *Calluna vulgaris* 'Mrs. Ronald Gray'
2 *Erica carnea* 'Leslie Sparkes'
3 *E. cinerea* 'Tom Waterer'
4 *Calluna vulgaris* 'Jan Dekker'
5 *C. vulgaris* 'Gold Haze'
6 *Erica cinerea* 'Glencairn'
7 *Calluna vulgaris* 'Hammondii Aureifolia'
8 *Erica carnea* 'Springwood Pink'

(Cordyline australis), which may be killed to the ground in bad winters; and variegated holly.

Attention to detail is meticulous. An isolated conifer is underplanted with dwarf daffodils for early-spring color. A dark bay is lit by the silver-gray foliage of *Santolina chamaecyparissus* and *Helichrysum petiolatum*, which survives the milder winters.

Heather beds

When the garden was started several decades ago, the planting consisted of numerous cultivars of spring heath *(Erica carnea)*. Today, there are over 200 differ-

ent kinds of heaths and heathers in flower every month of the year.

The heathers form generous spreads of color, with flowers in harmonious shades of red and pink through to contrasting white. The foliage effects are lovely, too. There are cultivars with gray, gold, and bronze leaves. And the long-lasting seed heads of some species are very decorative.

Given the right conditions, heathers are easy to care for and soon spread into a weed-suppressing ground cover. Because the seed heads of callunas and summer-flowering ericas are attractive, deadheading is not usu-

ally necessary. In spring, trim off the faded spikes of these and winter-flowering heathers, close to the foliage. A few particularly vigorous cultivars need to be cut back hard before spring growth starts.

Though heathers can be included in a mixed border, they look particularly attractive when grouped together in beds of their own to form carpets of color. No less than three of a kind should be grouped together to create a massed effect.

The island beds of heathers are separated by narrow paths of gravel, grass, or shredded bark.

The beds are edged with logs, and heather cultivars are planted toward the center of the mounded beds so they can creep downward.

Compatible shrubs are planted alongside the heathers. Among them are shrubby potentillas, the variegated *Euonymus fortunei* 'Emerald 'n Gold,' *Skimmia japonica* 'Rubella,' spiky phormiums, and fountain dracaena. All of these have distinctive foliage that contrasts with the small scalelike leaves of the heathers.

Important, too, are the many slow-growing dwarf conifers, often regarded as the classic partners for heathers. Their conical and rounded vertical forms and colorful foliage rise gracefully above the mounds of heathers.

Some beds have a front edging of ground-covering perennials such as *Heuchera micrantha* 'Palace Purple' and *Polygonum affine*. Clumps of snowdrops and *Crocus tomasinianus* give a lovely show in late winter and spring.

▶ **Golden cypresses** The conical shape of *Chamaecyparis lawsoniana* 'Lanei' adds height to the heather beds and brightens the somber shelterbelt of pines and spruces.

▼ **Multilevel planting** Specimen shrubs, like the red-flowered *Fuchsia magellanica* on the right, combine with conifers of various shapes and sizes to create plantings of continuous interest. The densely planted garden contrasts strongly with the open fields beyond.

Wall shelter

A dark Irish yew is planted near the house, softening one of its rear corners. It provides a contrast to the white walls. Shrubs that need protection also find a home here. There are several blue ceanothuses and a crimson-flowered, lemon-scented bottlebrush *(Callistemon citrinus)*.

In addition to colorful seasonal annuals in pots and hanging baskets, there are half-hardy twin olearias in large pots.

Also close to the house, where the ground drops toward the heather beds, are various ground-covering perennials battling for supremacy. Mossy saxifrages, white *Iberis sempervirens*, purple aubrietas, dwarf hypericums, and dainty maiden pinks *(Dianthus deltoides)* all intermingle with *Cotoneaster horizontalis* and prostrate junipers.

▲ **Tapestry of color** Leaf and flower colors and textures are in abundance. They range from heather mounds to spires of conifers and dense banks of trees and shrubs.

▼ **Secluded corners** Closely mowed grassy paths meander through the island beds to sunny sitting areas. Heathers and an acidifying mulch of shredded bark suppress weeds.

▼ **Specimen shrubs** Flowering and foliage shrubs mix with heathers and conifers. They include golden potentillas, blue-green rue, variegated hollies, and ribbed-leaved viburnums.

A COLORFUL SPRING GARDEN

**Acid-loving plants frequently
form spectacular spring displays and then remain
attractive for the rest of the year.**

Two major groups of acid-loving shrubs, rhododendrons and camellias, put on their impressive show of flowers in the spring. Because these evergreen shrubs include so many different species, hybrids, and cultivars, in mild climates blooming often begins in late winter or even earlier, as with *Camellia japonica* and *C. sasanqua,* which in the Deep South may open their first flowers in the fall.

The camellias have finished flowering by late spring, but rhododendrons — which begin their show as early as March — may continue blooming into early, mid-, and even late summer, depending on the species. Both these types of evergreen shrubs thrive in dappled shade and require acid soil, although camellias are slightly more alkaline tolerant than rhododendrons.

Some people forgo the attraction of a garden planted for year-round interest in return for a shorter period of intense color and dazzling beauty. The well-established garden shown here, with its blaze of color, is an example of a garden planned to be at its most spectacular in spring.

Site and layout
This typical suburban backyard garden is rectangular and level. This dictates a symmetrical, formal garden design: a rectangular central lawn edged with narrow borders. A small patio next to the house overlooks the garden, and at the back is the garden's centerpiece: a brick-paved area with an ornamental pool and a statue. The pool is semicircular, in contrast to the surrounding straight lines.

The soil is acid, rich in humus, and well drained — ideal for acid-loving plants, such as azaleas and camellias. The climate is temperate, with warm, damp summers and cool, but not harsh, winters. Mature trees in the garden and in adjacent gardens provide light shade and some shelter from cold spring winds.

Shade is important for this planting plan, as the shrubs generally favor woodland conditions and their flowers tend to lose their color if exposed to full sun. Shelter also comes from the brick boundary walls, the house itself, and the high brick building that adjoins the back of the garden.

Flowers and foliage
Second only to spring flowers is the emphasis on evergreen foliage, which creates a subtle contrast of leaf texture, form, size, and color once flowering is over. Evergreens also provide privacy, important in a built-up suburban setting.

◄ **Spring flowers** In this garden's mild climate, camellias and rhododendrons flower from late winter to early summer, wreathing the garden's perimeter with a succession of blooms. Later, the evergreen foliage gives an impression of cool and restful seclusion.

The plants at the garden's outer edges are tall, as are those near the house, to make maximum use of the limited planting space and reinforce the feeling of enclosure.

There is also a pleasing contrast between informal and formal plantings. The shrubs, trees, and herbaceous plants around the sitting areas are left to grow as their nature dictates, intermingling to create a narrow band of "woodland." Rows of clipped, spherical boxwoods on either side of the lawn establish a visual rhythm and add to the garden's formality.

Dark green is the dominant color — one that seems especially cool in hot weather. The spring colors are largely the pinks, crimsons, and whites of azaleas, camellias, and complementary tulips. However, the choice is not dogmatic, and occasional blues and yellows are included for contrast and to invigorate the whole design.

Rhododendrons and azaleas
Rhododendrons and azaleas are a favorite source of spring color in moist, acid soil. These compact, long-lived shrubs need little, if any, pruning. They require no support and are rarely troubled by pests or diseases. They blend well with other acid-loving shrubs and are easy to fit into a mixed shrub planting. A wide choice of cultivars and hybrids is available.

It should be noted that botanically speaking there is no distinction between azaleas and rhododendrons, since both groups of shrubs actually belong to the same genus, *Rhododendron*. Nevertheless, gardeners tend to reserve the name "rhododendron" for the larger and leathery-leaved evergreen species, such as *Rhododendron maximum*, our native rosebay. They distinguish as azaleas the deciduous *Rhododendron* species, as well as the finer-leaved evergreen types. Because nurseries commonly follow the practice of distinguishing azaleas from rhododendrons, this book will too, when identifying plants by common names.

Kurume azaleas, with their relatively small leaves and small but

densely packed flowers, are prominent in this garden. They originated in Kurume, Japan, in the 19th century and were introduced to the West in the 1920's. Since then, many new cultivars have been bred, especially in the United States.

The evergreen Kurume azaleas here include 'Apple Blossom,' with pale pink, white-throated flowers; the compact, bright crimson 'Hinodegiri'; and the clear pink, tall-growing 'Hinomayo,' originally obtained from the emperor's garden in Tokyo and one of the hardiest Kurume azaleas.

The garden also contains many Vuykiana hybrids, which were bred in a Dutch nursery named Vuyk. They produce relatively large blooms. The upright-growing 'Palestrina,' a distinctive green-tinted, white-flowered azalea, is used to cool down the pinks and reds of the Kurume azaleas as well as to break up their horizontal mass.

Evergreen shrubs

In zone 8 gardens such as this one and southward, camellias make natural partners for azaleas, with their similar floral color range, similar cultivation needs, and overlapping flowering time. The large, glossy foliage and more upright growth habit add interest to massed azaleas and create contrast in scale.

Because the proportion of camellia flowers to foliage is less than that of azaleas, camellia leaves help to "cool down" the flowering scene. A few early-flowering camellia cultivars lead up to the main display, which comes in mid- and late spring here.

Flowering dogwood (*Cornus florida*) helps to balance the color scheme, the light airiness of its white bracts relieving the denser color of the azaleas. This dogwood also has brilliant fall foliage and red fruits.

The huge, handlike, rich green leaves of fatsia, grouped near the house, add contrast in size and form. Though their fall flowers are insignificant, their berries — first green, then black — provide subtle interest. A compact, low-growing × *Osmarea burkwoodii* is also included for its fragrant white flowers and dark evergreen foliage.

Podocarpus macrophyllus, occasionally called the southern yew, is an unusual coniferous tree, with dense spirals of long, narrow leaves. Suited only to warm climates, it is planted here against a wall, where its foliage contrasts with the broad-leaved plants and its upright growth habit is easily accommodated.

Loquat (*Eriobotrya japonica*), with huge chestnutlike leaves and an upright growth habit, is also

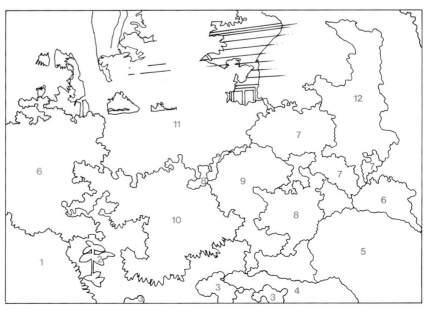

SPRINGTIME COLOR

Nothing brings such a delightful display of color to a garden in the spring as a mass of azaleas. They are a perfect choice for acid soil and grow equally well in large containers or raised beds.

A mixture of deep green foliage from trees, shrubs, and ground cover provides the ideal foil for the many shades of pink, which blend well together. A tall-growing deep pink camellia follows the color theme and adds visual height to the grouping. Like the azaleas, camellias thrive in dappled shade.

1 × *Osmarea burkwoodii*
2 Toadshade (*Trillium sessile*)
3 Strawberry geranium (*Saxifraga stolonifera*)
4 English ivy (*Hedera helix*)
5 Boxwood (*Buxus sempervirens*)
6 Rhododendron hybrid
7 Kurume azalea (*Rhododendron* 'Hinodegiri')
8 Kurume azalea (*Rhododendron* 'Hinomayo')
9 Kurume azalea (*Rhododendron* 'Apple Blossom')
10 Vuykiana azalea (*Rhododendron* 'Palestrina')
11 *Camellia japonica* 'Mathotiana'
12 *Camellia japonica* cultivar

planted against a wall. This provides the extra warmth it needs to thrive and produce its pear-shaped edible fruit in summer.

Ground-cover plants

The combination of ground-cover plants is typical for a semishaded spot with well-drained yet moisture-retentive acid soil. None of the plants are showy, in keeping with the temperate-climate woodland flora.

English ivy is used as a basic carpet, through which clumps of other plants grow. The ivy is always cut back when it encroaches beyond its allotted space or starts to climb trunks or stems. Some ferns, such as the lady fern *(Athyrium filix-femina)*, the acid-loving evergreen deer fern *(Blechnum spicant)*, and the evergreen but tender holly-leaved fern *(Cyrtomium falcatum)*, provide a graceful yet small-scale feeling of height. They are especially effective overhanging the paving.

The ornamental strawberry *(Duchesnea indica)* has typical semievergreen trifoliate leaves, but yellow — not white — flowers. The fruits are small and flavorless. Here, it vies with ivy for space, as both plants are vigorous.

The most unusual of the ground-cover plants is strawberry geranium *(Saxifraga stolonifera)*. Though more often seen as a houseplant in hanging baskets, where its plantlets on long, threadlike stolons are displayed to best advantage, it is hardy as far north as zone 6 and makes good ground cover as far south as zone 10.

The leaves, marbled and veined with white, add subtle contrast to

◀ **Shades of red and pink** In a corner of the garden, a ball-shaped evergreen boxwood has a calming effect on the pink color scheme of rhododendrons and azaleas and on a crimson camellia of treelike proportions. Large trees overhead cast dappled shade.

▲ **Stone statue** A charming statue makes a low-level focal point in the narrow border by the house. It draws the eye to tall architectural shrubs, including a large fatsia and the unusual *Podocarpus*, with its spirals of dark green leaves. On the left a huge camellia is in splendid bloom.

the all-green plants and brighten the dark areas under the shrubs. They also create an attractive rufflelike edge to the beds, visually unifying the garden and smothering weeds with their dense, quick-growing leaf cover.

Navelwort *(Omphalodes verna)* grows among the ivy. This long-lived plant forms dense carpets of heart-shaped leaves and intensely blue flowers like tiny forget-me-nots, to which the plant is related.

Trillium, or wake-robin, is a North American spring-flowering herbaceous perennial. Each stem carries a three-petaled flower above a whorl of three leaves. Trilliums grow too slowly to rank as ground cover but make graceful specimen plants.

Spring-flowering bulbs include bluebells — which pick up the

▲ **Chinese cranes** Nestling beneath the camellia, a pair of ornamental cranes create yet another focal point and underline the Oriental influences in the garden. They are set in a ground cover of ferns and strawberry geranium *(Saxifraga stolonifera)*.

contrasting blue of the navel-wort — and massed lily-flowered tulips, which are planted in single-color drifts of pink and white that continue the color theme of the shrubs.

Paths and paving
The beds are edged in a single row of brick, making mowing and weeding much easier and creating visual continuity between the brick sitting areas. The edging extends to the planting spaces for the clipped boxwoods, thus

◀ **Oriental flavors** The large brick-paved sitting area has many Oriental elements, from Japanese azaleas and camellias to Japanese holly ferns *(Cyrtomium falcatum).* Even the ball-shaped boxwood shrubs are of Asian origin, and the two stone elephants that guard the entrance to the semicircular pool emphasize the theme.

▼ **Dappled shade** Delicate azalea blooms appreciate the shade cast by the overhanging branches of the taller shrubs — direct sun would scorch and fade the flowers. A good mixture of azaleas is planned for successional flowering; the shrub in the background is still in bud.

Lily-flowered tulips in the foreground echo the overall pink color scheme.

helping to emphasize their essential formality.

A small change of level helps to give a sense of enclosure to the rear patio. Though only one brick high, the shallow brick platform between the pool and sitting area defines the area against the flatness of the surrounding lawn and the planted borders.

Features and focal points
Much of the planting is Oriental in origin, and Oriental ornaments — a lantern and a pair of crane statues — repeat that theme. But because the setting is so obviously Western, Occidental ornaments are included: a reproduction of a classical statue and urns at the entrance to the rear sitting area, and another statue as a point of visual interest in the shrubbery.

An ornate cast-iron table with a Victorian grape motif and cast-iron and wooden benches and seats are painted an unusual soft sea-green. An Oriental teahouse lantern rests on the table, encapsulating the successful merging of Eastern and Western plants and features.

GARDENING ON SANDY SOIL

The problems of a small lot and quick-draining acid and sandy soil can be solved by choosing plants compatible with the size and the soil.

Sandy soil can be very acid and may become more so unless properly and regularly managed. Such soil is light and well drained. It warms up rapidly in spring, dries out quickly, and in fall cools down sooner than soils of denser texture do. The main problem with acid, sandy soil is the rate at which essential nutrients, especially nitrates and potash, are lost with the drainage water.

As a result, sandy soil is commonly deficient in nutrients and low in moisture, producing weak, sparse plant growth like that found on the dunes of a beach or in a pine barren. In areas of high rainfall and on fast-draining slopes, calcium leaches out of the soil, producing manganese and iron deficiencies. Eventually salts accumulate below the topsoil in an impervious layer known as a hardpan. This impedes drainage, which makes the soil even more acidic.

Soil improvements

It is important to increase the water-holding capacity of sandy soil, whether it is acid, neutral, or alkaline. This is best done by digging in large quantities of organic materials, such as garden compost or a thoroughly decomposed manure. Regular and generous fertilization is also essential; nitrates and potash, in particular, must be applied annually. Liming will help to reduce soil acidity.

Sandy soil truly benefits from mulches, which conserve moisture and keep the soil cool in hot weather. Organic mulches, such as shredded bark or spent mushroom compost, improve the soil structure if they are lightly forked in at the end of the growing season, with fresh mulches being laid the next spring. Dense ground cover also acts as a moisture-conserving mulch; although it does not improve the soil structure, it can prevent erosion.

A linear garden

The primary challenge of a long, narrow garden is to counteract the tunnellike feeling that such gardens often have. Formal geometric layouts are often successfully used to divide narrow gardens into a series of "rooms," but a more informal layout can work equally well.

The secret is to include three or four main features, or points of interest — a lawn, a patio, and shrubbery, for example — and lay them out so that the curves flow into one another, while still dividing the lot crosswise.

This garden, which has acid, quick-draining sandy soil, is a

▼ **Small-scale acid lovers** A rock-strewn, gravel-covered alpine meadow planted across the entire width of the narrow garden alters the whole perspective. Modest-size trees, including purple-leaved maples, add height to the landscape of rock plants and a garden pool.

◄ **Trough gardens** Stone or cast-concrete troughs, set up on bricks for better viewing, hold collections of sempervivums and other alpines. Diminutive conifers, in pencil and dome shapes, repeat the planting scheme of the large rock garden on a miniature scale. Container gardening is useful for growing plants requiring soil of a different type from that found in the open ground.

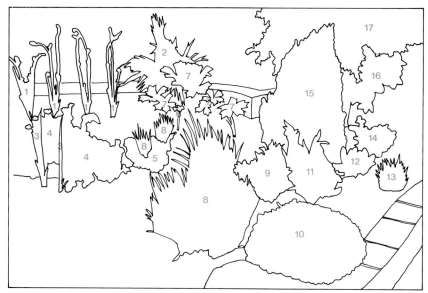

POOLSIDE PLANTING

The pool, incorporated into the rock garden, is well placed beside the patio to give a good view of the plants and water wildlife. The plan above identifies the main plants in the spring view on the left.

1 Royal fern *(Osmunda regalis)*
2 *Narcissus*
3 Yellow flag *(Iris pseudacorus 'Variegata')*
4 Marsh marigold *(Caltha palustris)*
5 Water mint *(Mentha aquatica)*
6 Candelabra primula *(Primula pulverulenta)*
7 Rodgersia *(Rodgersia podophylla)*

8 Cattail *(Typha minima)*
9 Cow parsley *(Chaerophyllum)*
10 Boxwood *(Buxus sempervirens)*
11 Yellow lady's slipper orchid *(Cypripedium calceolus pubescens)*
12 Silverweed *(Potentilla anserina)*
13 Dwarf iris *(Iris hybrid)*
14 Herbaceous potentilla *(Potentilla atrosanguinea)*
15 Oriental arborvitae *(Platycladus orientalis 'Conspicua')*
16 Green dragon *(Arisaema dracontium)*
17 Variegated kerria *(Kerria japonica 'Variegata')*

good example of what can be achieved in a small and potentially awkward space. The long, narrow 25 ft x 100 ft (7.5 m x 30 m) back garden faces south and is surrounded on three sides by well-established mixed conifer hedging. The hedges, which provide shelter and complete privacy, are pruned back close to the property line to make the most of the width of the garden.

The garden is divided informally into four basic areas. Closest to the house is a patio of multicolored paving slabs laid in an abstract shape.

The second section, stretching across the width of the lot, is a large rock garden. Set within this is an ornamental pool; a small pump-operated feeder stream connects the upper level of the pool with large basins below.

A gravel path, curved to give a diagonal view of the garden, leads toward the third section, just beyond the rock garden. There, a curved lawn narrows into a bottleneck shape before opening out into more generous proportions. In an informal bed located between the lawn and one boundary hedge are some slow-growing trees, shrubs, and woodland perennials.

Stone troughs and terra-cotta pots, clustered around the patio, hold collections of slow-growing saxifrages, sempervivums, and dwarf daphnes. Containers of choice alpines are brought under plastic-roofed cover during winter; in this way the plants are protected from wet weather, which might cause rot, and yet are still exposed to the cold temperatures they prefer.

The rock garden

This feature was created out of naturally occurring rock combined with stones that were bought and trucked to the site. Large boulders were set singly at strategic points; then clusters of smaller rocks and short lengths of drystone wall were arranged into gently irregular contours and outcrops.

The soil for the rock garden was made by mixing soil from the excavation of the pool with equal parts, in volume, of gravel and sphagnum peat. This blend assured the combination of moisture and good drainage that alpines demand.

A 1 in (2.5 cm) mulch of gravel was spread over the rock garden to create the feeling of an alpine scree. The gravel reduces weeding to a minimum; it also helps to preserve soil moisture and keep the soil cool, even in summer, as alpine plants prefer. In addition,

with the mulch, the bases of the alpine plants stay dry and are protected from the rot that often attacks them outside their natural high-mountain habitat.

The ornamental pool

Pools in small gardens can look artificial unless they are carefully designed to fit naturally into the garden layout.

This pool was dug out in a free-form shape and lined with 6 in (15 cm) of concrete. The edges are finished with rocks to hide the concrete and create pockets for moisture-loving plants. As the planting is small in scale, the pool appears larger than it actually is.

The pool has three depths, from shallow shelves around the edge to a center 2½ ft (75 cm) deep, so as to accommodate waterside and aquatic plants, which need different depths of water. The deepest section of the pool holds some fine koi carp, and frogs and newts have found their own way into the water.

All the aquatic plants are grown in perforated plastic containers to control their spread. In spite of this, the water lilies thrive to such an extent that they need

▲ **Poolside color** The evergreen garland flower (*Daphne cneorum* 'Eximia') grows only 6 in (15 cm) high but sprawls over a wide area in the moist ground by the pool. In early summer it is smothered with rose-pink richly scented flowers, which stand out prominently in the green foliage.

regular cutting back to prevent their leaves from covering the entire surface of the pool.

The pool is fed primarily from water collected off the house roof — the runoff from a water barrel is piped to the pool. When needed, this is supplemented with a hose.

General planting

The planting is a mixture of the

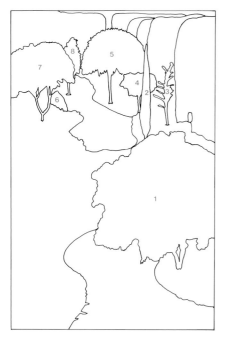

SPECIMEN TREES FOR A SMALL ACID-SOIL GARDEN

Most of the ornamental trees (shown opposite and identified in the plan) are ideally suited to a modest-size lot. Maples have attractive foliage and elegant forms; they do particularly well in dry acid soil. The maplelike liquidambar, planted for its glorious fall foliage, is pruned back every year to contain its growth.

1 Japanese maple (*Acer palmatum* 'Atropurpureum')

2 Irish juniper (*Juniperus communis* 'Hibernica')

3 Sweet gum (*Liquidambar styraciflua* 'Variegata')

4 Golden full-moon maple (*Acer japonicum* 'Aureum')

5 Butterfly bush (*Buddleia alternifolia*)

6 *Thuja occidentalis* 'Rheingold'

7 Japanese maple (*Acer palmatum* 'Osakazuki')

8 Japanese maple (*Acer palmatum* 'Sango-kaku')

▼ **Japanese maple** The golden full-moon maple *(Acer japonicum* 'Aureum'), with its deeply cut leaves, is liable to sun scorch. In the shade and shelter of a conifer hedge, it lights up a dark corner.

▲ **Wall plants** While the Canadian hemlock *(Tsuga canadensis)* is a tall conifer, the cultivar 'Pendula' forms drooping branches above variegated *Heuchera sanguinea*. Blue *Phlox subulata* adds color.

widely available and popular — large hybrid tulips in clumps of separate colors in the rock garden, for example — and the rare, such as lady's slipper orchids near the lower pool.

The planting is scaled to fit in a modest-size garden, so no extensive pruning or removal is needed.

In winter there are daphnes, snowdrops, and the ornamental red bark of dogwood and *Acer palmatum* 'Sango-kaku.' Fall foliage color comes from Japanese maples, spring color from traditional bulbs and alpines, and summer interest from perennials planted around and in the pool — ligularias, hostas, irises, astilbes, and water lilies.

Trees and shrubs
A purple-leaved Japanese maple (*Acer palmatum* 'Atropurpureum') overhangs the pool. Its domed shape is a focal point for the pool and rock garden.

A superb golden-leaved maple (*Acer japonicum* 'Aureum') is equally arresting and competes for attention with a *Buddleia alternifolia* trained into a weeping standard and lightly pruned to maintain a striking formal outline. A pencil-slim Irish juniper is naturally formal and upright. The one large tree, a sweet gum, is pruned annually.

PLANTS FOR ACID SOIL

An acid soil that is fertile and moisture retentive can be more of a delight than a problem. It is the preferred soil of many beautiful plants.

Acid soil can be seen as a problem or as an exciting challenge and potential source of garden character. Luckily, some of our most beautiful garden plants thrive in this soil, and you can do much to improve the quality of even the poorest sandy acid soils.

Acid soils lack natural deposits of calcium or limestone. Many are acid because they are built up over an acidic bedrock. Others are a result of air pollution or chemical fertilizers. Cultivated soils tend to become increasingly acid with time, because of the acidity of manures, many composts, and plant remains. The most accurate way of determining the amount of acidity or alkalinity in the soil in your garden is to use a soil-testing kit.

The presence of certain wild plants, such as chickweed, blueberries, sedges, mountain laurel, or native rhododendrons, usually indicates an acid soil. Another clue is the color of *Hydrangea macrophylla* flower heads, which are pink or red in alkaline or neutral soils and blue in acid soil.

The effect of acid soil

Though a very acid soil — say, pH 4.5 or less — limits the range of plants you can grow, a moderately acid soil is actually beneficial. Most ornamental plants prefer a pH of 5.7 to 6.7, at which level the greatest number of nutrients, in the form of chemical elements, are available to the plants. Many plants that prefer neutral or alkaline soil will also tolerate this level of acidity.

Below 5.7, the more acid a soil is (the lower the pH), the less available are the three major elements — nitrogen, phosphorus, and potassium — that plants need to thrive. Calcium, an important minor element, also becomes "locked" into the soil, while other minor elements — iron, aluminum, and manganese — become too freely available and are then harmful to plant growth.

Types of acid soil

Acidity level is just one of many

▼ **Rhododendron splendor** A full range of brilliantly colored rhododendrons and azaleas can be grown in fertile, moist acid soil. Open woodland trees and foliage plants create the lightly shaded conditions in which these acid-loving shrubs thrive.

factors determining whether a plant will thrive in a certain soil. Equally important are the nutrient content, texture, and porosity of a soil — and whether it is free-draining or subject to waterlogging. "Sour" is a term many gardeners use to describe waterlogged soil, and such soils are often (though not always) acid.

Many sandy soils are acidic, often because they are mixed with peat. Of course, sandy soils may also be alkaline, as they commonly are in coastal areas or in the arid West. Many clay soils and loamy soils are also acid.

There are cool, moist acid soils over a high water table shaded by trees and hot, dry acid soils in full sun, like those found in pine barrens or dune areas. There are fertile acid soils, which may include decades' worth of decomposed leaves; and there are impoverished acid soils, such as those often found in urban gardens. A plant that thrives in one type may perish in another, even though both have the same pH.

Improving acid soil
Whatever type of acid soil you have, your goal should be to make it moisture retentive but well

▲ **Spring camellias** These shrubs thrive in slightly acid to neutral soil, light shade, and north-facing sites. They bloom as early as Christmas in mild-winter regions.

▼ **'Forest flame'** This cultivar of *Pieris formosa* needs a mild climate and acid soil. In spring it bears new red leaves and drooping white bell-shaped flowers.

drained, fertile and friable, and loosely open to a depth of 1½ ft (45 cm). Though it may seem contradictory, working in well-rotted compost or manure both increases the water-retentive capacity of thin, sandy soils and peat-based soils *and* improves the drainage of heavy clay soils. This treatment also improves and renews soil fertility — very important with thin, sandy acid soils.

Digging in organic matter is more immediately effective than mulching, but mulching is better than nothing, and combining both is ideal. An old but effective remedy for thin, sandy soils is to grow a green-manure crop of lupines for 2 years, leaving their nitrogen-fixing roots in the soil and digging in the top growth after flowering. Mow the top growth, chopping it into small pieces, before turning it into the soil with a rotary tiller.

Regular topdressings of lime, in the form of ground limestone or hydrated lime, raise the pH, but be careful in applying lime around acid-loving plants. Hydrated lime acts fast but can burn plants; ground limestone acts more slowly and is safer. Dolomitic limestone adds magnesium as well as lime. The exact amount of lime depends on the soil type: acid clay soils need more lime than acid sandy soils. As a general rule, apply 8 oz (200 g) of lime per sq yd/m once a year.

If you intend to dig in manure, wait at least a month after liming before doing so. Combining manure and lime releases ammonia, which can harm plants.

Acid lovers and lime

If you are determined to fight nature and grow acid-loving plants in alkaline soil, read the catalogs of specialty nurseries carefully.

▲ **Star of the show** Rhododendrons are undoubtedly the most popular of all acid-loving shrubs. Famous for their huge heads of spring or early-summer flowers, these evergreens come in a range of sizes, from ground-hugging to tree-size types, and in colors ranging from white through pastel shades to deep crimson and violet-blue.

Just because one species in a genus dislikes alkaline soil, it does not necessarily follow that all species do. Most *Erica* species dislike limy soil, but *E. carnea*, *E. cinerea*, *E. × darleyensis*, and *E. mediterranea* tolerate slight alkalinity. Most magnolias need a moderately acid soil, but a few, such as *Magnolia × loebneri* hybrids, will tolerate alkalinity too.

Even the stunning trumpet gentians have lime lovers and lime haters among their numbers. *Gentiana clusii* thrives on

limestone; the similar-looking *G. acaulis* needs an acid soil. One rhododendron, *R. hirsutum*, will put on a good show in alkaline soil, and the strawberry tree *(Arbutus unedo)*, a plant of the Ericaceae family, tolerates lime.

If your soil is alkaline and yet there are acid-loving plants you cannot do without, you can spot-treat the soil. Line the planting hole with moistened sphagnum peat and then fill in around the plant's roots with peat-enriched soil. This may allow the acid lover to flourish for an extended period of time, though the natural alkalinity will eventually leach in from the surrounding earth or with the irrigation water if that is alkaline. Regular doses of chelated iron, sold as a plant "tonic," may also benefit the out-of-place acid lover.

Raised beds of peat-enriched soil or retaining walls filled with acid soil are less vulnerable to leaching but are expensive to construct. They also dry out in hot weather. Large containers, such as half barrels, work on the same principle but are a cheaper and simpler alternative. It is a good idea to remove old soil annually from the top of the container and replace it with a fresh supply. Make sure that drainage in the container is adequate, and use rainwater, not tap water, for artificial irrigation.

Acid-loving plants

Whether a plant needs or simply tolerates acid soil is unimportant to most gardeners, provided that the plant flourishes and flowers well. It is true that some plants *must* have acid soils — azaleas, many heathers, and rhododendrons, for example. Others, such as camellias, are fine in a neutral or acid soil with no trace of lime.

Many plants — campanulas, peonies, roses, hydrangeas, and philadelphus, for example — will grow in a good range of soils on either side of neutral, provided the soil is well drained, deep, and reasonably fertile.

As a general guide, plants of the Ericaceae family — heaths and heathers (*Erica* and *Calluna*), *Rhododendron, Pieris, Gaultheria, Leucothoe, Enkianthus, Kalmia, Pernettya,* and so on — thrive in well-drained acid soil.

Some fruits, especially blueberries, will grow only on very acid soil; and gooseberries, blackberries, raspberries, cranberries, and red currants perform well in soils with a pH around 6.5. Most vegetables and herbs tolerate soils that vary from acid through neutral to alkaline, though parsley prefers acid soil.

Lastly, there are the tough survivors of the plant world that tolerate both extremely acid *and* extremely alkaline soil. This category includes juniper, mugho pine, black pine, yew, hawthorn, European birch, paper birch, beech, white poplar, aspen, Turkey oak, bur oak, holly, goat willow, privet, and elder.

Seasonal shrub color

Gardens with moderately acid, well-drained soil can provide

▲ Late-summer scene
Conifers and heathers are traditional partners in acid soil. Heathers form ground cover beneath pyramidal, mounded, or pillarlike dwarf conifers in this garden. The early-flowering heathers are almost over, while the first of the later-blooming cultivars are coming out. Given enough room and well-drained to sandy acid soil, heathers can be in bloom every month of the year.

▲ ▶ Fall display The large fothergilla *(Fothergilla major)* needs acid soil to bear its bottlebrush flower spikes in spring and its rich fall colors. It harmonizes well with a pink-flowered *Nerine bowdenii*.

▶ Late spring The acid-loving *Kalmia latifolia* bears large clusters of saucer-shaped flowers, which stand out nicely against the glossy evergreen foliage.

color and interest the year round. As a rule, evergreens are the key to winter interest. Choose from rhododendrons, camellias, elaeagnus, hollies, and heathers — the latter with gold, russet, and purple-tinged foliage, as well as green. Grow dwarf or full-size pine, juniper, and cypress in dry, sandy, or acid clay soils. Plant mahonia, chamaecyparis, yew, thuja, and silver fir *(Abies alba)* in acid clay soils.

Most rhododendrons and camellias flower in spring, but you can extend the season in both directions by careful selection of cultivars, and heather can be in flower every month of the year. Honeysuckle — climber or shrub — thrives in both heavy and light acid soils, and there are deliciously fragrant winter-flowering varieties in addition to spring- and summer-flowering types.

In an acid soil garden, flowering camellias signal the arrival of spring with their stunning pink, red, and white flowers and glossy dark green leaves. Though spectacular in a group on their own, they can also be underplanted with 3 ft (90 cm) high *Leucothoe fontanesiana,* a dwarf shrub with arching branches of willowlike evergreen foliage.

Rhododendrons make their presence known throughout the year with their evergreen foliage, but it is their large trusses of flowers in spring and early summer that give rise to eye-catching partnerships. Harmonious groups of color always look better than a jumble of different hues, so mix pink-flowering and red-flowering rhododendrons, and in front introduce lower-growing perennials with flowers of similar colors. Bergenias will echo the pink of rhododendrons, and the evergreen leaves of both could provide a backdrop for the purplish-red flowers of *Primula japonica* or soft pink *P. pulverulenta* — two acid-loving perennials that grow 2 ft (60 cm) high. *Pieris forrestii* is another evergreen shrub useful for associating with azaleas and rhododendrons. Its cascades of white urn-shaped flowers in midspring, followed by delicate pink and scarlet young leaves, contrast dramatically with the bold rhododendron blooms.

In dry, sandy acid soil, kerria and redbud *(Cercis)* give brilliant gold and rosy pink spring color,

respectively, followed in summer by gorse, tamarisk, genista, and sun and rock roses, and in late summer by hibiscus. In damp acid soil the mountain laurel *(Kalmia latifolia)* produces its showy clusters of pink flowers in late spring or early summer.

Roses thrive in slightly acid clay soil, as do viburnums, weigelas, mock oranges *(Philadelphus),* deutzias, witch hazels *(Hamamelis),* chaenomeles, potentillas, hypericums, and most magnolias — it is really a question of what to leave out rather than of searching for plants to include.

Hydrangeas, flowering in midsummer to early fall, will prolong the season of interest among acid-loving shrubs, and in acid soil the blue-flowered forms will be truly blue. A good partner for the popular lace-cap *Hydrangea* 'Blue Wave' is the tall, graceful shrub *Eucryphia × nymansensis,* which

▲ **Spring companions** White bottle-brush heads of *Fothergilla major* weave above bluebells and *Rhododendron yakusimanum,* whose rose-red buds open through pink to white.

▼ **Woodland planting** In dappled shade, pink and red rhododendrons share the moist acid soil with a footing of crimson candelabra primulas *(Primula pulverulenta).*

▲ **Cornish heath** The summer- and fall-flowering Cornish heath *(Erica vagans)* thrives in sandy acid soil and full sun; it is a robust plant that is hardy to zone 6. Here, the pink-flowered cultivar 'St. Keverne' blends its long sprays with the golden foliage of winter-flowering *Erica carnea* 'Aurea.'

◄ **Mountain heathers** Different cultivars of heather *(Calluna vulgaris)* weave a tapestry of color in a large open rock garden backed by dark green conifers. Native to Europe but naturalized in parts of the northeastern United States, heathers flower from midsummer to late fall. In this simulated mountain landscape, the heathers are joined by clumps of *Polygonum affine*, with lance-shaped dark green leaves and flower spikes of deep pink.

▼ **Feathery astilbes** At their best in moist, rich, and slightly acid soil, *Astilbe* x *arendsii* cultivars bear fluffy flower pyramids in white, cream, and shades of pink and red throughout summer.

▲ **Gentian trumpets** The fall-flowering *Gentiana sino-ornata* bears long-throated trumpets of startling blue, which are striped with white and dark blue pencil-slim markings. It needs humus-rich soil and partial shade.

▼ **Banks of rhododendrons** Magnificent rhododendrons are the best-known of all acid-loving shrubs and span the full color spectrum. Hostas and alchemillas stand at their feet.

▲ **Japanese camellias** Cultivars of *Camellia japonica* offer flowers from white to pink and red. All require light shade and moist acid to neutral soil. This specimen stands out with its golden-centered, white semidouble flowers.

bears eye-catching cream-white flowers.

For fall berries, grow cotoneasters, berberis, and pyracantha in acid clay, loam, or sandy soil; and in dry acid soil, include pernettyas as well. There are maples for most acid soils; box elder *(Acer negundo)* is particularly good in dry acid soil.

In open sites, various types of heather, flowering at different times and offering many foliage colors, can be used to create a tapestry-like effect.

Acid-loving perennials

There is also an amazingly wide choice of perennials suited to slightly acid clay soil: aconite, aster, geum, hosta, daylily, phlox, physostegia, rudbeckia, goldenrod, dicentra, geranium, astrantia, Solomon's seal, and so on.

Peaty, moist acid soils support crown imperial fritillary and Asiatic primulas in spring; then meconopsis, globeflower, *Filipendula rubra* 'Venusta,' *Iris kaempferi,* and astilbes, and ending with Japanese anemones in fall. For a splash of color in boggy acid soil, try ligularias, or golden rays — ragged orange or yellow daisies above huge rounded leaves.

For summer color in dry, sandy acid soil, choose from achillea, alkanet, golden marguerite *(Anthemis tinctoria)*, Italian aster, Stokes' aster, *Salvia* × *superba,*

echinops, sea holly, heuchera, flag iris, lupine, cupid's dart, foxtail lily, goat's rue, incarvillea, and balloon flower.

Rock gardens with acid soil are ideal for the blue gentians. Intense color also comes with lithospermums and lithodoras, whose prostrate stems are studded in summer with blue funnel-shaped flowers.

▲ **Spring heathers** *Erica carnea* tolerates some alkalinity in the soil; it does best in sun and well-drained soil. Cultivars come in white, pink, and red, with green or golden leaves.

▼ **Blue cover** The bright blue *Lithodora diffusa* 'Heavenly Blue' flowers from early summer on and spreads a wide carpet over rock gardens in neutral to acid soil.

PLANTS FOR ACID SOIL					
	NAME	**DESCRIPTION**	**HEIGHT**	**SPREAD**	**SITE**
TREES AND SHRUBS	*Acer negundo* (box elder)	Deciduous tree; bright green maple leaves; several variegated forms	30 ft (9 m)	15-20 ft (4.5-6 m)	Sandy, dry soil; sun or shade
	Calluna species (heather)	Evergreen shrubs; tiny leaves; white, pink, or purple flowers in summer and fall	4-24 in (10-60 cm)	4-30 in (10-75 cm)	Peaty/sandy soil; sun or light shade
	Camellia species (camellia)	Evergreen shrubs; glossy oval leaves; single or double flowers in white, pink, or red	7-10 ft (2.1-3 m)	5-7 ft (1.5-2.1 m)	Humus-rich soil; light shade
	Cercis siliquastrum (redbud, Judas tree)	Deciduous tree; heart-shaped leaves; rosy pealike flowers in spring; purple seedpods	15-20 ft (4.5-6 m)	10-15 ft (3-4.5 m)	Tolerates dry soil; sun and shelter
	Colutea arborescens (bladder senna)	Deciduous shrub; pale green divided leaves; yellow pea flowers; inflated seedpods	8 ft (2.4 m)	8 ft (2.4 m)	Tolerates dry soil; sun
	Erica species (heath)	Evergreen, usually dwarf shrubs; needlelike leaves; bell-shaped flowers	¼-20 ft (7.5-600 cm)	1-12 ft (30-360 cm)	Peaty/sandy soil; full sun
	Gaultheria species (gaultheria)	Evergreen shrubs; leathery leaves; small urn-shaped spring flowers; berries	8-48 in (20-120 cm)	8-48 in (20-120 cm)	Moist soil; semishade
	Kalmia latifolia (mountain laurel)	Evergreen spreading shrub; glossy leaves; clusters of white, pink, or red flowers	3-10 ft (90-300 cm)	4-8 ft (1.2-2.4 m)	Cool, moist root run
	Leucothoe fontanesiana (leucothoe)	Evergreen shrub; arching branches; semievergreen leaves; white flowers in summer	6 ft (1.8 m)	4 ft (1.2 m)	Well-drained soil; semishade
	Pieris species (pieris)	Evergreen shrubs; red young leaves; small waxy white flowers in spring	6-12 ft (1.8-3.6 m)	6-8 ft (1.8-2.4 m)	Peaty/sandy soil; light shade
	Rhododendron species (rhododendron, azalea)	Evergreen or deciduous shrubs; clusters of flowers, mainly in spring and summer	3-20 ft (90-600 cm)	3-16 ft (.9-4.8 m)	Moist peat; semishade
	Robinia species (locust)	Deciduous trees and shrubs; finely cut leaves; pealike flowers in early summer	6-30 ft (1.8-9 m)	6-15 ft (1.8-4.5 m)	Any soil, especially dry; sun
	Tamarix species (tamarisk)	Deciduous shrubs; graceful plumelike foliage; feathery pink flowers in late spring or late summer; wind resistant	10-15 ft (3-4.5 m)	10-15 ft (3-4.5 m)	Sandy soil; sun
PERENNIALS AND BULBS	*Adonis vernalis* (pheasant's eye)	Herbaceous perennial; fernlike leaves; golden bowl-shaped flowers in early spring	9-12 in (23-30 cm)	12 in (30 cm)	Moist soil; sun or light shade
	Cyananthus microphyllus (trailing bellflower)	Trailing perennial; narrow midgreen leaves; blue bellflowers in early fall	3 in (7.5 cm)	1 ft (30 cm)	Moist soil; sun
	Erythronium revolutum (trout lily)	Hardy bulb; white and brown mottled leaves; Turk's-cap-like white flowers with purple markings in spring	1 ft (30 cm)	6 in (15 cm)	Moist soil; light shade
	Gentiana sino-ornata (gentian)	Low-growing alpine that spreads into wide, grassy mats; deep blue flowers in fall	6-8 in (15-20 cm)	12-15 in (30-38 cm)	Deep, moist soil; semishade
	Incarvillea delavayi (hardy gloxinia)	Herbaceous perennial; deeply cut leaves; rose-pink flowers in early summer	2 ft (60 cm)	15 in (38 cm)	Moist acid or neutral soil; sun
	Lilium auratum (gold-banded lily)	Hardy bulb; tall stalks with narrow lance-shaped leaves; fragrant white flowers with crimson spots and central golden stripe on each petal in summer	3-9 ft (90-270 cm)	9-12 in (23-30 cm)	Well-drained, humus-rich soil; sun or partial shade
	Meconopsis betonicifolia (Himalayan blue poppy)	Herbaceous perennial; long green leaves; sky-blue poppylike flowers in summer	3-5 ft (90-150 cm)	1-1½ ft (30-45 cm)	Moist, well-drained soil; shade and shelter
	Trillium grandiflorum (trillium, wake-robin)	Rhizomatous perennial; pale green oval leaves; three-petaled white flowers in spring and summer	1-1½ ft (30-45 cm)	1 ft (30 cm)	Moist soil; shade

Gardening on alkaline soil

The main problem with alkaline soils is that they are commonly shallow, deficient in nutrients, and subject to drought. In the western states, where they are most common, alkaline soils frequently lie above a rocklike layer of calcareous material known as caliche, so that plant roots cannot penetrate more than a few inches. In such a situation, planting holes may have to be chipped out with a crowbar. Also, alkaline soils are commonly stony, with each digging operation bringing yet more stones and larger pieces of rock to the surface.

To garden successfully on very alkaline soil, it is essential to increase the depth of soil with bulky organic materials. These are generally acidic and thus help to reduce the lime content in the soil. Organic mulches — leaf mold, pine needles, or shredded bark — conserve soil moisture and also increase the depth of the topsoil. Even so, some plants fail to thrive on alkaline soil and develop stunted growth and yellowing leaves.

It is a waste of money and effort to attempt to grow plants that cannot tolerate your soil type. Acid lovers such as rhododendrons and camellias cannot thrive in alkaline soil, except as specimen shrubs in containers of acid potting mix. However, there are plenty of plants to replace them — crab apples and flowering cherries, blue ceanothus and pink mallows, lilacs and sun roses, junipers and yews, and clematises in all their variety. Numerous perennials and alpines also grow naturally on limy soils — valerians and pinks, gentians and sea thrift, New York asters, and all the silver and woolly-leaved foliage plants.

Drought-proof beauty The delicacy of fairy-duster's flowers belies this desert native's toughness.

SOUTHWESTERN STYLE

The secrets to successful gardening in the Southwest are innovative design and plants adapted to the chronic drought and poor, alkaline soil.

In most southwestern states, chronic — and often extreme — drought and poor, alkaline soil present major obstacles to successful gardening. Yet the Southwest is also a region of abundant sunshine and mild winters. Indeed, this region is a paradise for gardeners if they learn how to work effectively with the local climate and soil.

Pictured on the following pages are several gardens in Tucson, Arizona, which through skillful design have been brought into harmony with the surrounding desert. These outdoor spaces are attractive and comfortable the year round and yet require only an hour or so of weekly maintenance. In addition, these gardens are remarkably thrifty in their use of water, demanding only a small fraction of the irrigation needed to support conventional suburban landscaping in the arid southwestern climate. Such conservation is important to the health of the environment, and it may also translate into considerable savings in the gardener's water bills.

Southwestern soils

The soil in Tucson (and indeed throughout most of the arid West) tends to be rich in lime and thus strongly alkaline; in Tucson, a typical pH ranges from 8.0 to 8.5. Besides making the garden inhospitable to plants that need an acid or neutral pH, the amount of lime in southwestern soils leads to another problem. Rainfall is meager, an average of 11 in (27 cm) annually, and most of it falls in a few violent late-summer thunderstorms. The moisture from these storms may penetrate several inches or even several feet into the soil, carrying all sorts of dissolved salts (especially lime) with it.

The salts are left behind when evaporation off the soil surface draws the water back up out of the ground. Eventually the lime deposits collect into a rocklike layer of hardpan known locally as caliche. This layer may be only a few inches below the surface, and in such cases, planting holes may have to be excavated with a pick or iron bar. Deeper-lying caliche may also stunt plant growth,

---

▼ **Lush oasis** Turf has been reduced to a room-size carpet in this outdoor living space. Surrounding walls ward off dehydrating winds, and two hardy desert trees — a willowleaf acacia (left) and a Chilean mesquite (right) — furnish shade for the flowers and the trailing indigo bush *(Dalea greggii)* that spill out of planters beneath.

▲ **Native hardscape** Inspired by the stony-surfaced desert, these gardeners let hard surfaces — tile, concrete, and stucco — dominate. Boulders were brought in, and the pavement was poured around them so that the garden would seem to have spread itself over native desert.

since it generally presents an impermeable barrier to spreading roots. You can excavate caliche or try a less labor-intensive solution, like the one adopted by the owners of the garden pictured on pages 143 and 148. They built soil-filled raised beds 1½-2 ft (45–60 cm) high, so that their plants could have a deep root run despite the presence of caliche.

A final problem with many southwestern soils is their low organic content. Whereas a midwestern prairie soil may contain 5 percent or more humus by weight, in Arizona the organic content is more likely to hover at 0.1 percent. The lack of organic matter reduces the soil's fertility and robs it of its ability to retain whatever moisture is gained either through rainfall or irrigation — the water just washes through the soil.

Boosting the organic content of the soil with plenty of sphagnum peat, compost, or well-rotted manure will improve this situation. When preparing a new bed or replanting an existing one, spread the organic matter over the soil in a layer 2-3 in (5-7.5 cm) thick and then dig it in with a spading fork, turning the soil to a depth of at least 1 ft (30 cm).

Keeping beds covered with an organic mulch, such as shredded bark or wood chips, will also increase the soil's organic content, since the mulch turns into humus as it decomposes. Many southwestern gardeners, such as the owners of the landscape above and on pages 145-147, prefer crushed rock or pebble mulches, believing that they harmonize better visually with the stony surface of the surrounding desert. Although such inorganic mulches do not add humus to the soil, they do assist water conservation. Both rock and organic mulches block the evaporation of water from the soil surface. Mulch also promotes root growth by keeping the soil cooler; a 3 in (7.5 cm) layer of leaves will keep the soil beneath it as much as 18° F (10° C) cooler than the bare earth nearby.

Limiting the lawn

Many gardeners newly arrived in the Southwest try to reproduce the landscapes they left behind in the North or Midwest — and so they cover their new lots with lawn. In fact, many kinds of turf grasses will thrive in a southwestern setting, but traditional choices such as hybrid Bermuda grass flourish only with constant lavish irrigation. In Tucson it was the custom to administer 1 in (2.5 cm) of water to the lawn at least twice a week — until it was recognized that lawn irrigation was a major cause of the depletion of the region's aquifer and the consequent water shortage.

Experienced southwestern gardeners now recognize that turf is a luxury in their region and treat it accordingly. The creators of the garden pictured on page 143 have included a Bermuda grass lawn in their design — but the total expanse is about the size of a large Persian carpet. Indeed, the turf serves much the same purpose, providing a short, soft "rug" on which the owners can sit or stretch out.

A lawn may be a more practical landscape treatment in rainier and cooler upland regions of the

Southwest, but even there it is usually best to plant a drought-tolerant native turf, such as buffalo grass, crested wheat grass, or blue grama, rather than some thirsty exotic like Bermuda grass. Because the native grasses have only recently been adopted for use in lawns and are not yet thoroughly domesticated, they furnish a wilder, less finished look. But improved strains, such as 'Prairie' buffalo grass, are beginning to appear, and these typically exhibit greater uniformity of growth and color.

Most of all, remember that a lawn is not only impractical for the dry soil of the Southwest but is also burdensome in terms of maintenance. Pushing a mower under the desert sun is hard, unpleasant work and may actually be physically dangerous for older gardeners.

An oasis of color

All the gardens pictured in this chapter rely on the same basic design principle. To reduce the need for irrigation, limit the time spent on maintenance, and better integrate the domestic landscape into the surrounding desert, the gardeners have left their properties' perimeters to semicultivated expanses of native vegetation. Gardening here is limited to the removal of obtrusive plants. Intensive cultivation has been limited to small, enclosed "oases" placed adjacent to the house in areas of the landscape that see constant use.

The walls surrounding these oases act as windbreaks, blocking the desiccating desert winds. This reduces the need for irrigation of the plants within, while also enhancing the comfort of people relaxing in the garden.

Hardy desert trees such as mesquite *(Prosopis),* palo verdes *(Cercidium),* and acacias *(Acacia)* are planted along the walls to further break the wind and provide some shade. Their delicate foliage does not block the intense southwestern sunlight but does filter it, providing a gentler habitat at ground level for shrubs such as prostrate indigo bush *(Dalea greggii)* and fairy-duster *(Calliandra eriophylla)* and drought-tolerant perennials such as the native red-flowered autumn sage *(Salvia greggii)* and the many species of native penstemons.

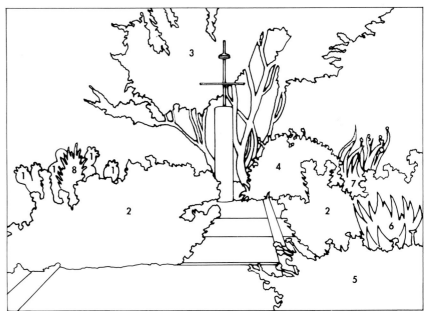

OPEN-AIR SHOWER

Utility combines with beauty here in a small nook set off to the side of the pool pictured on the preceding page. The sculptural object in the center is an outdoor shower set in a small pavement of fast-draining cobbles.

1 Prickly pear *(Opuntia engelmannii)*
2 Euphorbia *(Euphorbia biglandulosa)*
3 Foothills palo verde *(Cercidium microphyllum)*

There swimmers may wash before and after their dip. The surrounding plants are dryland species, which provide shade and flowers and flourish with occasional irrigation from a drip system.

4 Autumn sage *(Salvia greggii)*
5 Perennial verbena *(Verbena peruviana)*
6 Century plant *(Agave univittata)*
7 Penstemon *(Penstemon parryi)*
8 Feathery cassia *(Cassia artemisioides)*

Water features

A swimming pool is a common feature of the Tucson oasis gardens. If equipped with a floating cover to seal it when not in use, it loses relatively little water to evaporation. If the bottom of the pool is painted black, the water's surface becomes a mirror to reflect views of far-off mountains and helps to connect the garden to the surrounding countryside.

In smaller gardens a modest fountain serves the same purpose

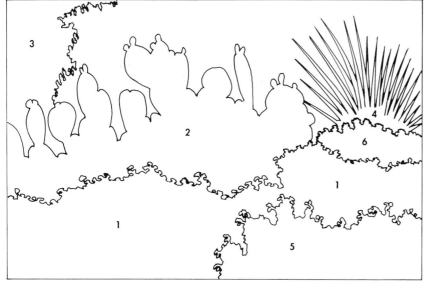

A DESERT BORDER

Yet another aspect of the swimming pool garden pictured on pages 144 and 145, this mixed border of dryland shrubs and perennials offers a variety of foliage and flowers. Blackfoot daisy and autumn sage blossom nearly year-round with occasional irrigation. The shrubs are chiefly spring blooming, but their grayish and bluish foliage provides a soothing backdrop for the perennials at other seasons.

1 Blackfoot daisy *(Melampodium leucanthum)*
2 Prickly pear *(Opuntia engelmannii)*
3 Hardy cassia *(Cassia nemophila)*

4 Desert spoon *(Dasylirion wheeleri)*
5 Autumn sage *(Salvia greggii)*
6 Purple prairie clover *(Petalostemon purpureum)*

as a pool. The tiny basin pictured on page 148 supports an exotic-looking bouquet of papyrus *(Cyperus papyrus)* and water hyacinth *(Eichhornia crassipes)*. When a small recirculating pump is turned on, the water is lifted in a low jet, whose splashing makes the entire garden scene seem much cooler.

Adapted plants

The most important step toward success in southwestern gardening is to cultivate plants naturally adapted to the local climate. This involves giving up the moisture- and cool-loving garden plants inherited from northern European gardeners and looking closer to home for garden inspiration.

Many southwestern nurseries have begun stocking more native plants in recent years. Cacti and succulents such as agaves are obvious choices for a desert garden, and their effect doesn't have to be one of spiny austerity.

There are spineless and nearly spineless types of prickly pear, for example, which will pose no threat to garden visitors. Depending on the cultivar, the pads may take on shades of blue or purple, contributing to an inviting garden picture. On page 148, as an example, a blue-green Indian fig *(Opuntia ficus-indica)* is wreathed with the cerise blossoms of *Bougainvillea* 'Barbara Karst.'

This bougainvillea demonstrates another point — that not all adapted plants are natives. Bougainvillea is a South American vine or shrub that needs irrigation during the spring growing season. But it blooms best under the stress of drought in summer. Likewise, the Chilean mesquite *(Prosopis chilensis)* performs as well in Tucson as the native velvet mesquite *(P. velutina)*. Both species can send their roots deep into the ground (to 175 ft/52.5 m or more) and so can forage for their own water throughout most of the year.

Lusher, water-loving plantings also have their place in southwestern gardens. A bouquet of pansies may be set out to furnish wintertime color, or a cluster of zinnias can be planted in springtime. If cultivated in pots, such accent plants require very modest (though frequent) watering. Like a fountain, the annuals supply an

air of luxuriance with little investment of time or money.

Waste-free watering

Within the oases, irrigation is provided by drip irrigation systems. Sprinklers are rarely used in the Southwest, since they waste more water than they deliver to the plants. In the arid atmosphere of that region, half or more of the drops from the sprinkler may evaporate before they

▲ **Foundation planting** An upright willow pittosporum *(Pittosporum phillyraeoides)* casts a tracery of delicate foliage on a stucco wall. Spread out beneath are (left to right) scarlet autumn sage, euphorbia, agave, and verbena.

▼ **Local color** The designer of this pool has given it a rocky, jagged profile borrowed from the mountains in the background. A coyote cut from sheet metal dips his muzzle in the water — as if at some desert spring.

◄ **Exotic hardiness** The splendor of *Bougainvillea* 'Barbara Karst' makes a persuasive case for the place of exotic flora in the desert garden. A native of the tropics, the evergreen bougainvillea is remarkably drought tolerant once established.

▲ **Lush desert** Bluish pads of prickly pear and rosettes of *Agave vilmoriniana* make a striking setting for the scarlet bougainvillea blossoms. To the right a Chilean mesquite shelters a fountain filled with papyrus; the basin's edge is wrapped with trailing indigo bush.

▲ **Container plantings** Graceful terra-cotta containers filled with annuals — Transvaal daisies *(Gerbera jamesonii)* and chrysanthemums *(Dendranthema)* — add a note of color to this corner of pavement. Such plantings offer flexibility, as they are easily changed to suit the gardener's mood.

hit the ground, and on a slope, much of the rest may run off downhill and so be lost as well. Also, by wetting the whole soil surface, sprinklers encourage the germination of weed seeds.

A drip irrigation system delivers water through small tubes and emitters (hidden underneath the mulch in these gardens) to the base of the garden plants, so none is lost through evaporation. Drip irrigation delivers water slowly. These systems operate at low pressure, releasing the water drop by drop, at a rate at which the soil and plant can absorb it. The net result is a reduction in water use of up to 75 percent; even in the heat of summer, the owners of the garden shown on page 143 operate the drip system only about 15 minutes a day.

However, a drip irrigation system can achieve this level of economy only when plants have been selected and grouped according to their need for irrigation. Extremely drought-tolerant plants,

such as agaves and euphorbias, should be set in one bed, while plants with a greater need for moisture — annual flowers, for example — are grouped elsewhere. Setting moisture-loving annuals among drought-tolerant native perennials means that half the plants must be overwatered if the other half are to survive. This wastes water, and it ensures that part of the garden will be unhealthy and unattractive.

Skillful southwestern gardeners supplement their irrigation by "harvesting" natural moisture. Deep-rooted plants, such as trees and shrubs, are set in shallow depressions. The rain that falls on the house roof is fed from the downspouts through rock-lined "washes," or channels, into the planting basins. The water soon disappears down into the soil, but the resulting moisture can persist in the subsoil for many weeks. Even in Tucson, this may supply all the water that a desert tree needs.

BEHIND CITY WALLS

**The problems of thin, alkaline soil and
a minimum of space can be overcome to produce
a peaceful haven of lush, exotic plants.**

In a small urban garden every bit of space is precious, and each ornament, feature, plant, and piece of furniture has to be chosen and sited with special care. In a way, creating a small garden is more challenging than laying out a large one, in which mistakes can be absorbed into or disguised by the general greenery. In a large garden you can always look in another direction or walk around a corner to another place. But truly successful small gardens have a uniquely precise beauty that is well worth taking care to achieve.

This small rectangular back garden faces south and belongs to a Victorian house in a busy coastal town. About 20 ft x 60 ft (6 m x 18 m) in size, the garden has high stone walls on three sides and the back wall of the house on the fourth side.

The soil is thin, alkaline, and fast-draining. Prolonged severe frosts are a rarity in this mild maritime climate, and the high walls provide additional shelter as well as privacy. The white-washed house and the garden walls reflect light and heat into the garden, creating a brighter, warmer microclimate.

Layout and design

The enclosing walls make this a very private garden, and the use of water features, large-scale ornaments, and selected sculptural specimen trees and shrubs gives it the feeling of an exotic retreat.

The layout creates an illusion of space in a small area, while at the same time adding an element of mystery and surprise. Though the garden is in the middle of a bustling town and overlooked by other houses, the aim of total seclusion with a minimal loss of sunlight has been successfully achieved.

The lot is divided crosswise roughly in half to give two interconnected "rooms": the one close to the house is paved with brick, and the other has a turf floor. The "rooms" are separated and defined by curving shrub beds set at right angles to the garden walls.

Shrubs form an informal arch that frames the view of the second "room." This visual stopping point breaks up the rectangular shape and helps to disguise the smallness of the garden.

Raised, curved planting beds hug the garden walls in the lawn

---

▼ **Leafy retreat** Designed for privacy, this small, leafy garden can be admired from the house as well as at close range. The mellow brick pavement makes a handsome backdrop to intense planting.

"room," and a narrow area of paving borders the end wall — this makes mowing easier and provides a resilient surface on which to stand plants in tubs and pots. Nearer the house, a raised ornamental pool abuts the garden wall and is surrounded by lush vegetation and variegated ivies. These climb like a mantle around a wall-mounted water fountain in the shape of a lion's head.

Views into and out of the garden are treated carefully. From the ground-floor windows it is impossible to see the entire area beyond the arch, so the imagination is allowed to roam free. The pool, however, has been sited deliberately where it can be seen and heard from the house. The house itself is not visible from the seat at the back of the garden, which is secluded in its own leafy retreat.

Artificial features

Most of the masonry and garden ornaments are secondhand, so that they lend an air of age to the garden and harmonize with the Victorian architecture. Materials came from architectural salvage yards or were rescued from demolition sites.

The stone from which the retaining walls were made was recycled from demolished buildings and walls. This was done partly in the interests of economy; local masonry supply companies sell such salvaged materials at a fraction of the cost of freshly quarried stone. But the decision to use salvaged materials also made sense aesthetically. The local quarry that furnished the stone for the wall enclosing the property was long ago mined out and closed. Only by reusing stone removed from nearby building sites was the garden's present owner able to match the original.

The stone retaining walls at the rear of the garden are built in relaxed, flowing curves with roughly rounded tops. In the more formal walls of the ornamental pool, the corners are

◀ **Garden sentinels** At the transitional point between the brick flooring and velvety lawn, a laurel tree and a fountain dracaena narrow the perspective and lead the eye on an imaginary voyage of discovery.

built up with brick to get an exact right-angled geometry, with rougher stone set into panels in the sides. Precast concrete paving slabs are set along the walls' tops to make a coping wide enough to double as a sitting area.

The old brick in the paved area nearest the house is set in sand without mortar, with intentional irregularity and unevenness. This too adds a traditional, well-established feel to the garden.

Bricks of different colors were used in this pavement to create a Persian-carpet-like effect. Outer bands and an inner central stripe of blue-gray brick set off the red brick filling the area in front of the pool. Adjacent paving has a random mix of dark blue and red bricks. Square brick pavers of dark blue-gray mark the end of the paved area.

The brick arch in the wall above the pool draws attention to the lion's head waterspout, making a suitably theatrical setting for the pool itself.

Clusters of glazed stoneware jugs interspersed with plants are pleasantly grouped against the house wall, and old terra-cotta roof finials are used as decoration in the rear garden "room." A stone greyhound crouches at the farthest spot from the house, giving an illusion of distance.

▲ **Greyhound replica** A stone greyhound, as inscrutable as a carving from an Egyptian tomb, gazes from its shady corner beneath gnarled tree trunks and long trailing vines.

▼ **Walls of greenery** Tall shrubs and mature trees festooned with climbers create solid green walls in a restful garden "room" with a floor of manicured lawn.

COLOR AND FORM

The plants around the pool area and along the boundary walls make excellent use of form as well as color.

1 English ivy (*Hedera helix*)
2 Impatiens (*Impatiens wallerana*)
3 Lobelia (*Lobelia erinus* 'White Lady')
4 Lobelia (*Lobelia erinus* 'Red Cascade')
5 Spider plant (*Chlorophytum comosum* 'Vittatum')
6 *Hosta elata*
7 *Hydrangea macrophylla*
8 Hemp palm (*Trachycarpus fortunei*)
9 Lobelia (*Lobelia erinus* 'Color Cascade Hybrids')
10 Ivy-leaved geranium (*Pelargonium peltatum* cultivar)
11 *Mahonia x media*

12 Male fern (*Dryopteris filix-mas*)
13 Lily (*Lilium* hybrid)
14 Fountain dracaena (*Cordyline australis*)
15 Honeysuckle (*Lonicera japonica*)
16 *Clematis x jackmanii* 'Superba'
17 Hanging baskets with *Lobelia* 'Color Cascade Hybrids' and petunias
18 Canary Island ivy (*Hedera canariensis*)
19 Umbrella plant (*Cyperus alternifolius*)
20 English ivy (*Hedera helix* 'Glacier')
21 Yellow flag (*Iris pseudacorus*)
22 Variegated Canary Island ivy (*Hedera canariensis* 'Variegata')
23 Zonal geranium (*Pelargonium x hortorum*, red-flowered cultivar)
24 Water lily (*Nymphaea* hybrid)

Planting plan

The most striking feature of this garden is the natural archway made by a topiary of clipped Portuguese laurel (*Prunus lusitanica*) and a fountain dracaena (*Cordyline australis*) — strange partners, perhaps, but very effective. Fountain dracaena is a native of New Zealand and hardy only in the mildest regions (zone 9 or 10), where it will grow to treelike proportions. While both plants are evergreen, there is a strong contrast between the rounded tapestry-like formality of the laurel and the gaunt sword-shaped leaves of the dracaena.

The Portuguese laurel is hardier, thriving to zone 7, and is excellent for hedging and topiary, thriving in shallow alkaline soils. White-variegated forms also exist.

Shrubs include lace-cap and mop-head hydrangeas, both of which thrive in seaside conditions. As well as giving long-lasting color throughout summer, the flowerlike bracts dry naturally on the stalks, assuming subtler hues and remaining attractive well into winter. In alkaline soil the hydrangeas remain blue only with annual applications of chelated iron, and even so the color is less intense than that of hydrangeas grown in acid soils.

The evergreen mahonias are indifferent to soil type and grow just as well in shallow alkaline soils as in deep clay. They provide year-round interest with their attractive spine-edged leaves and cheerful yellow flowers in spring.

The inclusion of a pieris in the shrub border is an optimistic attempt at defying nature. A pieris, like a rhododendron, demands an acid soil that is both moisture retentive and deep. Even after applications of chelated iron and irrigation with pH-neutral rainwater rather than the region's alkaline tap water, the pieris will never reach its full potential nor unfold its young, glossy red leaves and drooping clusters of lily-of-the-valley-like flowers. It would thrive and flourish if planted in a large tub filled with acid potting soil, however.

A slow-growing purple-leaved Japanese maple provides a lacy touch; its delicate pinnate leaves make a pleasant contrast to nearby horizontal junipers.

Climbing plants include the stunning large-flowered *Clematis x jackmanii* 'Superba,' which hangs in a curtain of purple near the seat, and sweetly fragrant honeysuckle. A jungle effect is created by a Virginia creeper, which hangs in long strands from an ancient apple tree near the boundary and fills the rear garden with brilliant crimson in fall.

Both large- and small-leaved variegated ivies cover the walls. Their densely overlapping leaves create a hedge effect, although they take up minimal space.

Herbaceous perennials that thrive in shade include hostas, ferns, Solomon's seal, and daylilies. Mature clumps of hostas look sculptural, with leaves radiating boldly from a central point. The graceful arching stems of Solomon's seal soften the brick.

Hanging baskets and pots brim over with colorful geraniums, petunias, lobelias, impatiens, and nasturtiums wherever space allows. Other temporary summer displays include the water-loving umbrella plant (*Cyperus alternifolius*), whose elegant upright growth contrasts with the rounded leaves of nearby water lilies. Green- and white-striped spider plants (*Chlorophytum*) also spend

▶ **Pool basin** The raised pool and the lion's head wall-fountain are reminiscent of classical Roman models. The walls of green ivies are entirely in keeping with the illusion, as is the floor of worn brickwork.

the summer months out of doors in the garden.

Maintenance

This coastal soil is alkaline and poor, which makes it hard for many plants to obtain essential nutrients, so annual applications of peat, organic fertilizer, and compost are needed. Deep mulches of the same materials or shredded bark help to retain moisture and improve the texture of the shallow soil.

A small garden with such intense planting needs fairly intensive care. The watering of potted plants during the summer is a daily commitment, as are feeding and deadheading. The hanging baskets need water several times a day in hot spells; the raised beds also need regular watering and feeding throughout summer — this sandy coastal soil is fast-draining and dries out quickly.

Tender plants are taken indoors every fall and planted or repotted in spring. Plants in pots, such as the geraniums and hydrangeas, are moved around, sharing the benefit of light; such nurturing pays off, as this sort of rotation allows color to be introduced to shady spots.

Routine tasks such as mowing the lawn take place during the growing season. In early spring a great deal of pruning must be done to keep the plants in scale with the compact garden and to prevent tall plants from shading out their smaller neighbors. The Virginia creeper would quickly swamp the space if not cut back; the tangle at the rear of the garden, with the creeper hanging down liana style, is a carefully tamed wilderness. The topiary is clipped regularly to maintain a bushy head, and the clematis is pruned hard in late winter to encourage flowering.

▶ **Paving pattern** The mellow brick paving is laid without mortar, in rectangular but irregular bands. Dark blue pavers echo the curve of laurel and fountain dracaena where the second garden "room" begins.

A CLEMATIS GARDEN

Queen of the climbers, the magnificent clematis revels in alkaline soil and in sun or shade — and its other needs, though definite, are easily met.

No garden should be without a clematis or two. They can be in flower from late winter until fall, depending on the cultivar, displaying their magnificent and exotic blooms over a long period. They will clothe walls and fences, climb over pergolas and arbors, or clamber up through large shrubs and trees. Some will even scramble over the ground, covering old tree stumps and mounds.

Clematis stems are weak, but they attach themselves to any available support by twisting their thin but tough leafstalks around it. On flat, smooth surfaces, provide clematis with a plastic or wooden trellis.

Some gardeners complain that clematises are difficult to grow. It is probably true that the species and their cultivars are easier to establish than the large-flowered hybrids, but there is no mystery surrounding clematis cultivation.

It is also said that clematises like their roots in shade and their heads in sun, but a few (including the spring-flowering *Clematis alpina* and *C. montana)* grow happily on shaded north-facing walls; others with delicate flower colors fade when exposed to full sun. In warm and sunny sites, provide shade over the root area by covering it with pavers or a stone slab, or plant a shallow-rooted evergreen foliage shrub, such as lavender or rosemary.

Lime lovers
Clematises are greedy feeders, and they demand fertile, deep soil with plenty of organic matter. They truly flourish in alkaline soil. Good drainage is essential, but copious watering during the growing season is also necessary. Clematises grown against the base of a fence or in a tiny pocket taken out at the foot of a wall derive little benefit from natural rainfall. They need deep watering — in hot weather at least every other day. In open ground, give clematises an annual mulch of well-rotted manure or compost, with a little lime mixed in for acid and neutral soils.

Pruning clematises
Different types of clematis have various pruning needs, depending on the flowering pattern.
Group 1 comprises early-flowering species clematises, such as *Clematis alpina*, and their cultivars. No pruning is needed other than cutting out dead or overcrowded shoots and shortening

---

▼ **Clematis hybrids** In spectacular bloom for many summer months, clematis cultivars flourish in limy, alkaline soil. Most like their roots in cool shade and their heads in bright light.

▲ Gravel cover A pathway of pale gravel is easy to install and maintain. It is also fast-draining, absorbs heat, and reflects light. It lends a Mediterranean look to the colorful planting in a small urban garden.

◄ 'Perle d'Azur' The large-flowered clematis hybrid 'Perle d'Azur' bears a profusion of flowers throughout the summer. It needs hard pruning in early spring.

shoots that have outgrown their allotted space, after flowering has finished.

Group 2 contains the large-flowered hybrids that bloom in early summer and midsummer, such as 'Nelly Moser' and 'Madame le Coultre.' Their blooms are born on shoots produced in the previous season, and only unwanted growth should be trimmed away after flowering. Old plants *can* be pruned back to healthy wood in late winter or early spring, but this will curtail the following summer's flowers.

Group 3 includes late-flowering species, such as *Clematis viticella*, and those large-flowered hybrids like the Jackmanii types that bloom in late summer and fall. They carry their blooms on shoots produced in the current season; they should be pruned

An evergreen hedge of × *Cupressocyparis leylandii* conifers spans the top end of the garden, concealing a small compost pile and a play area for children. In front are a variety of shrubs, including green-and-white variegated dogwood, valued for its attractive red branches during winter.

A stone bench provides an attractive focal point at the top of the garden, backed by a weeping specimen of the willow-leaved pear *(Pyrus salicifolia* 'Pendula') and a white rugosa rose. Potentillas, yellow-green *Euphorbia characias wulfenii,* and peonies add red and yellow highlights.

The pool is stocked with water lilies and marsh marigolds *(Caltha palustris).* It is edged with silvery *Senecio cineraria, Potentilla fruticosa,* and a prostrate blue juniper.

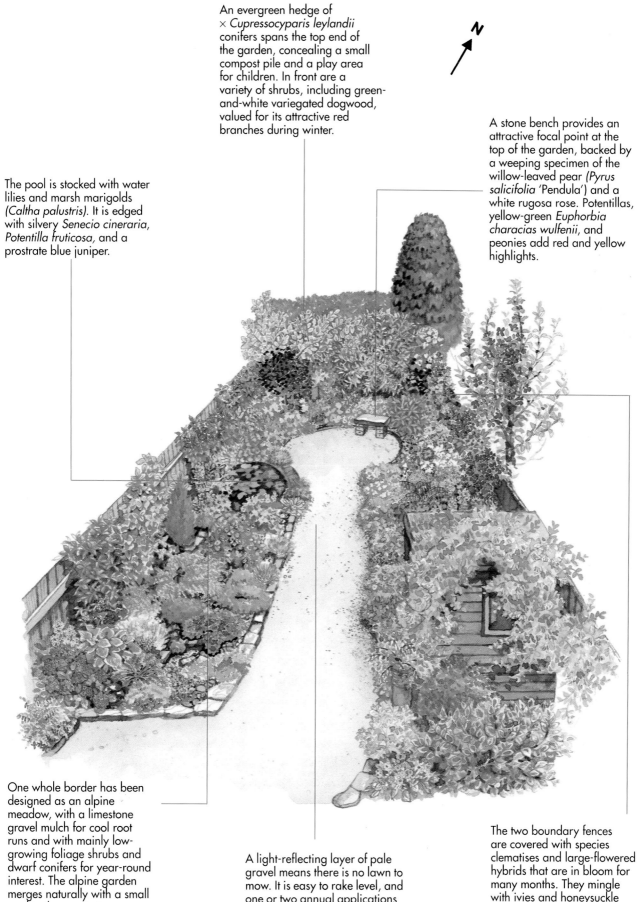

One whole border has been designed as an alpine meadow, with a limestone gravel mulch for cool root runs and with mainly low-growing foliage shrubs and dwarf conifers for year-round interest. The alpine garden merges naturally with a small pool in the sunniest corner of the garden.

A light-reflecting layer of pale gravel means there is no lawn to mow. It is easy to rake level, and one or two annual applications of herbicide maintain its pristine appearance. Grass is difficult to grow in shady gardens, and gravel makes an attractive and trouble-free alternative. Every few years this area is refreshed with a new coat of gravel.

The two boundary fences are covered with species clematises and large-flowered hybrids that are in bloom for many months. They mingle with ivies and honeysuckle above a border densely filled with lime-loving perennials that include phlox, Jacob's ladder, fuchsias, New York asters, and common thrift *(Armeria maritima).*

▲ **Old-fashioned clematis** Cultivated since the 16th century, *Clematis viticella* is a slender but vigorous climber. Its cultivar 'Abundance' bears veined red-purple flowers in summer and early fall.

back hard, to a pair of strong-growing buds on the shoots, 3 ft (90 cm) or less from the ground in early spring.

Planting clematis in a garden
The garden featured here is an urban garden with alkaline soil, about 70 ft (21 m) long and surrounded by boundary fences up to 7 ft (2.1 m) high. Shaded by nearby buildings and trees, the garden has been designed around a central pathway covered with pale-colored pea gravel. This cover is easy to maintain, reflects sun and

heat, and provides a startling and effective contrast to plants in the surrounding borders.

Many different clematis cultivars cover the boundary fences and create a long-lasting display from spring through to late fall. In early spring the pale blue *Clematis alpina* comes into flower. It is a relatively slow-growing type and consequently needs little pruning. It often has a second, more modest flowering period in summer, when its blue-gray silky seed heads appear.

The summer-flowering hybrid 'Ernest Markham' is grown in a tub near the house. Its large petunia-red flowers appear until fall.

On the north-facing fence near the house is a specimen of *Clematis tangutica* climbing a laburnum tree. Its lantern-shaped bright

yellow flowers appear from late summer until fall and are followed by silky seed heads. The yellow spring flowers of the laburnum and the later-flowering clematis clothe this shady corner in bright color for many months.

Also near the house is the white-flowered hybrid 'Madame le Coultre.' This flowers profusely from early summer to early fall on shoots produced the previous year; it is lightly pruned after flowering has finished. Occasionally, it is pruned back hard to two strong buds in early spring, and it then produces one major display in midsummer.

The lavender-blue clematis 'Elsa Spaeth' grows in the long border, above the pool. It is treated like 'Madame le Coultre,' sometimes trimmed lightly after flowering, in early fall, and sometimes pruned hard in winter.

Farther along, *Clematis texensis* 'Gravetye Beauty,' which has crimson bell-shaped, spreading flowers, sprawls over a viburnum bush. This less hardy clematis flowers on shoots of the current year and is cut back hard each spring; the top growth is clipped in fall so that the winter-flowering viburnum underneath can be seen.

Many different clematis cultivars clothe the southwest-facing fence. They include *Clematis viticella* 'Purpurea Plena Elegans,' with its large, double lilac-purple flowers paling toward the center. Its flowering period overlaps with that of its neighbor, the light blue 'Perle d'Azur.'

Also here is the vigorous *Clematis viticella* 'Abundance,' with wine-red flowers, scrambling up through a neighboring apple tree. Next to it is the free-flowering shell-pink 'Hagley Hybrid,' in constant bloom from early summer to early fall. Nearby is another *C. viticella* cultivar, 'Royal Velours,' which has velvety purple blossoms. All are pruned like *C. texensis* in early spring.

Clematis companions
One long border, edged with paving slabs, has been designed as an alpine garden. It is planted with low-growing rock plants, which are brightly colored in summer, and with near-prostrate conifers for year-round interest. The latter include easy-growing and lime-loving junipers, such as

Juniperus communis, the wide-spreading *J. × media* 'Pfitzerana,' and the low-growing *J. squamata*.

Silver-leaved plants introduce some contrast. The dwarf artemisia (*Artemisia schmidtiana* 'Nana') forms a mound of finely cut silvery leaves; senecios and gray-leaved and variegated helichrysums nestle alongside hostas; and bright aubrietas spill over onto the flat stones.

For winter color there are clumps of the low-growing and spreading evergreen *Euonymus fortunei* 'Emerald 'n Gold,' whose leaves are tinged with pink in winter. A yellow-variegated ivy, *Hedera helix* 'Buttercup,' clambers over the fence, hiding the clematis stems.

At the far end of the garden, a high hedge of × *Cupressocyparis leylandii* forms a good backdrop for a wide, curving border dominated by a silver willow-leaved pear (*Pyrus salicifolia* 'Pendula') weeping over a stone seat.

Mixed border

Sunny and sheltered, the far border is a pleasant mixture of alkaline-loving shrubs and perennials. Variegated philadelphus, red-leaved berberis, and a number of dogwoods (*Cornus*) are planted at the back, with the ivory-white shrub rose 'Nevada' for contrast.

Red and yellow colors are displayed here, from golden daffodils and red, yellow-edged 'Queen of Sheba' tulips in spring to *Helianthemum* 'Jubilee' (primrose-yellow) and 'Double Red' in early summer. Red and golden daylilies rise above a front planting of red-flowered potentillas, verbenas, and yellow pansies.

Blue and pink border

The southwest-facing border is stocked with blue, pink, and mauve flowers that nicely match the colors of the clematis growing on the fence. They include phlox, ranging from white through pale and deep cyclamen-pink to lilac; Oriental poppies; New York asters; fuchsias; Jacob's ladder (*Polemonium caeruleum*); and lavender.

To the front are geraniums, veronicas, pansies, blue-leaved rue, and silvery mats of alpine dianthus spilling over the gravel.

Late spring brings a dramatic display of tall, almost black fritillaries planted with black parrot tulips. In fall, a white- and yellow-flowered hybrid honeysuckle by the shed bears brightly colored (but inedible) orange berries.

▲ **Focal points** The shady sitting area by the house offers close views of the clematis border and of a stone seat by a weeping silver pear farther down the garden. Light and heat are reflected by the light-colored gravel.

▼ **Reds and yellows** Backed by red berberis and green and variegated dogwoods, red roses and honeysuckles bathe in the sun, rising above ground-covering clumps of golden potentillas and yellow pansies. Silver-leaved foliage plants temper the colors.

Plants for shade

The area adjacent to the house is refreshingly cool and shaded with many evergreen and spring-flowering plants, providing pleasant views from the house windows. A pink-flowered ornamental currant *(Ribes sanguineum)* stands by a large stone trough, which is filled with alpine flowers — saxifrages — that will bloom in winter in this particular garden's mild climate.

Christmas roses, bergenias, and the variegated *Arum italicum italicum*, with its curious flower spathes, are all evergreen perennials that are ideal for shade. They mix happily with miniature spring bulbs, including winter aconites, tiny hoop-petticoat daffodils *(Narcissus bulbocodium)*, and light and dark blue dwarf irises.

During the summer months, containers and hanging baskets of bushy and trailing fuchsias, ivies, wax begonias, and impatiens add bright, vibrant color to this shaded area.

▲ **Alpine beauties** Clumps of blue trumpet gentians and bellflowers *(Campanula carpatica)* bring summer color to an alpine meadow of gray and silver foliage plants and dwarf conifers.

▼ **Pool planting** Gray, silver, and blue foliage surrounds a small pool stocked with water lilies and marsh marigolds. Pink-flowered cranesbills *(Geranium endressii)* add spots of color.

LIME LOVERS

Some plants dislike alkaline soils, but there are many more that thrive in areas rich in calcium or lime.

Gardeners with limy or alkaline soil may think they have a problem. Many important plants — such as rhododendrons and most heathers, camellias, magnolias, and Japanese maples — cannot grow in alkaline soil. But many plants tolerate some alkalinity, and several positively thrive on it.

In alkaline soil, displays to rival those of acid-loving rhododendrons can be created with shrubby and climbing hydrangeas (although blue-flowered varieties turn pink and red), aucubas and cotoneasters, cherry laurels and sweet-scented honeysuckles. Skimmias, mahonias, spireas, and the snowberry bush *(Symphoricarpos albus)* also thrive on lime.

Nowhere are trees like beech, hornbeam, hawthorn, and mulberry as fine, especially in their fall foliage display, as in alkaline soil. And given warmth and shelter, the Judas tree *(Cercis siliquastrum)* will also do well.

The yew and common juniper both grow naturally in alkaline soil. Their many garden cultivars look good among the lime-tolerant winter-flowering heaths *(Erica carnea* and *E. × darleyensis)*. For summer color, plant the brilliant yellow-flowered Spanish broom *(Spartium junceum)*.

Flowering cherries and bulbs are happy in alkaline soil, providing many opportunities for spring combinations of forget-me-nots, wallflowers, pansies, lungworts, and primroses.

The incomparable pasqueflower *(Pulsatilla vulgaris)* will naturalize in alkaline soil. Plant pasqueflower on a sunny bank or

▲ **Alkaline partners** Growing wild, especially in limestone cliffs, common scabiosas and old-fashioned pinks are lifelong companions. Here, the garden types of blue *Scabiosa caucasica* share the alkaline soil with a strongly scented cottage pink, *Dianthus × allwoodii.*

▼ **Maltese cross** The scarlet flower heads of campion, or Maltese cross *(Lychnis chalcedonica)*, are even more brilliant in alkaline soil. They form a good partnership with the lemon-yellow flat heads of yarrow *(Achillea filipendulina 'Coronation Gold')*.

▲ Early-spring color
Stinking hellebore
(Helleborus foetidus) grows
wild in alkaline grasslands,
its fingerlike leaves providing
year-round foliage interest.
In early to late spring, purple-
tipped green flowers rise
over this leafy base, making
a perfect partner for lungwort
(Pulmonaria saccharata)
with silver-spotted foliage
and pink funnel-shaped
blooms, which turn blue as
they mature.

▲ Neutral soil Lupines and
foxgloves dislike both
strongly acid and strongly
alkaline soils, doing best in
deep and well-drained
neutral soil. Yellow species
daylilies *(Hemerocallis)* and
scarlet Oriental poppies
favor the same soil
conditions, although they
are more tolerant of lime
and drought.

◄ Lime life Russian sage
(Perovskia atriplicifolia)
thrives in alkaline soil and is
particularly happy in seaside
gardens. Its tall, downy stems,
set with gray-green leaves
that smell of sage, are topped
in late summer with sprays
of violet-blue flowers. They
complement the clear pink
hooded flowers of penstemon
perfectly.

◀ **Alkalinity indicator** Gray- or silver-leaved plants usually enjoy the perfect drainage associated with limestone soils. Here, the woolly foliage of *Stachys byzantina* 'Silver Carpet' provides a thick mat of soft, tongue-shaped leaves, the ideal foil for the dangling scarlet flowers of the hardy *Fuchsia magellanica.*

Alongside, an old-fashioned lavender *(Lavandula angustifolia)* matches bluish flowers with gray foliage in a classic cottage garden mixture.

▲ **Tolerant fire thorn** At home in alkaline or acid soil and in sun or partial shade, and tolerant of air pollution, the evergreen fire thorn *(Pyracantha)* produces billowing clouds of small creamy white flowers in early summer. It associates well with lime-loving perennials — such as the ferny-leaved *Achillea filipendulina,* with its clear yellow flat heads, and the tall-stemmed, gray-leaved *Verbascum* 'Gainsborough.' In fall, fire thorn bears huge clusters of berries.

▲ **Froth of white** The free-flowering annual baby's breath *(Gypsophila elegans)* is at home in alkaline soil. It creates an airy base for the spikes of blue, mauve, and pink larkspurs *(Consolida ambigua)*.

▶ **Violet companion** The large viola family thrives in a variety of soils and situations. The horned violet *(Viola cornuta)*, a true perennial, favors alkaline soil, where it will grow up to 1 ft (30 cm) tall and produce a succession of blooms (white in the cultivar 'White Perfection') throughout summer. Here, it partners the fragrant quartered blooms of an old-fashioned gallica rose.

◀ **Prairie fantasy** Ornamental grasses bring a distinctive quality to any group of plants and usually do well in alkaline soil. The lovely centerpiece here is the 3 ft (90 cm) tall Chinese fountain grass *(Pennisetum alopecuroides)*. Its graceful arching form and bottlebrush flowers, appearing in late summer and fall, contrast with the substantial green and gold-striped leaves of tender scarlet-flowered canna and the impressively tall annual *Nicotiana sylvestris*, with huge lyre-shaped leaves and clusters of scented white flowers.

in a rock garden, perhaps with helianthemum, aubrieta, arabis, and candytuft.

Taller wildflowers, such as *Campanula glomerata, Geranium sanguineum,* and ox-eyed daisy, make good border plants. Don't forget the Mediterranean herbs with gray or silver leaves, such as rosemary, thyme, and lavender — many of these love the perfect drainage of alkaline soils.

The red valerian *(Centranthus ruber),* which flowers abundantly on limestone cliff faces, also flourishes in the poorest and driest of alkaline garden soils. You can temper its fiery color with golden kniphofias, silvery lamb's ears *(Stachys byzantina),* or yellow-green lady's mantle, all of which favor alkaline soil.

Clematis associates

Clematises do for alkaline soil what rhododendrons do on acid ground — provide a stunning display of magnificent colors. They are a diverse group of plants, varying in flowering season from late winter through summer to fall, with blooms in all colors except bright red or orange. They have many growth habits, from climbing, through sprawling, to almost bushy. Some also have decorative feathery seed heads. All too often these marvelous plants are grown in lonely splendor on trelliswork or walls. In fact, they look very attractive growing among other plants.

The most familiar clematises are the large-flowered hybrids. Often vigorous and growing quite tall, they bloom too high up when grown on a house wall. Instead, grow them up through a small tree or large shrub, where their ultimate height depends on that of their partner. Further growth will tumble back to eye level.

Lower-growing hybrids, such as the pink 'Hagley Hybrid,' combine well with stiff-stemmed shrubs, such as ceanothus, common lilac *(Syringa vulgaris),* and the taller hydrangeas.

The lantern- or bell-shaped flowers of many species clematises look best when viewed head-on or from slightly above. These types can be grown as cascading arrays over low walls or through smaller shrubs, including viburnums, deutzias, and roses. Species clematis need little or no pruning, so partnerships with roses that need annual pruning may not work — the rose canes could not be cut without injuring the clematis stems.

Some species clematises, such as *Clematis texensis,* can even be trained through woody ground-cover plants and over tree stumps.

▼ **Close relations** Clematis hybrids, such as petunia-red 'Ernest Markham' and violet 'Mrs. N. Thompson,' make a glorious show grouped with the daintier yellow flowers and silvery seed heads of *Clematis tangutica.*

▲ **Clematis support** *Clematis montana rubens* adds subtle color to the evergreen glossy foliage of golden-leaved ivy (*Hedera helix* 'Buttercup'). Ivies are self-clinging and provide ideal support for the weak clematis stems.

▶ **Pergola cover** For a pillar or pergola, choose the less vigorous clematis types, so that they remain at an enjoyable eye level. Pillar roses and honeysuckles make suitable partners.

▼ **'Nelly Moser'** The popular 'Nelly Moser' clematis flowers in early summer and again in early fall. Like the fragrant nicotianas, it does best in light shade; otherwise the flowers fade.

PLANTS FOR ALKALINE SOIL

**Success with alkaline soil is simply a
matter of growing the right plants; the choices
include many beautiful species and hybrids.**

Certain garden plants such as camellias, rhododendrons, and many heathers strongly dislike alkaline soil and will not survive for long in it. Other plants intolerant of alkaline soil conditions never reach their full size or potential beauty, even with rigorous mulching and feeding — instead, they remain weak, with yellow foliage.

Rather than fight against nature, choose from the many beautiful plants that thrive in alkaline soil, and from the large number of easy-care plants that tolerate most soils, including alkaline ones.

Understanding alkaline soil

Alkaline soils are most common in our western states, but they may occur wherever there is a substantial concentration of lime — calcium carbonate — in the

soil. Such a soil may take several forms, such as alkaline clay, or a loam or sandy soil infiltrated with limestone, caliche, or occasionally chalk. By definition, alkaline soils all have a high pH, ranging from 7 upward.

There are advantages and disadvantages to alkaline soils.

Advantages Alkaline soils are well drained; waterlogging is not a problem, even in the wettest weather. Such light, dry soils warm up more quickly in spring than heavy, wet soils, so sowing and planting can take place earlier.

Most turf grasses prefer alkaline conditions. As a result, soils of that type support some of the most beautiful lawns. Also, vegetable crops usually perform better in moderately alkaline soils.

Disadvantages Because alkaline soils occur most commonly in the arid or semiarid West, their

fast-draining quality can make a garden exceptionally vulnerable to drought. Humus — the organic matter in the soil — acts like a sponge to absorb and retain water, keeping it in the soil and available to plant roots. Calcium carbonate (lime) speeds the decomposition of vegetable matter, robbing the soil of humus, so calcium-rich, alkaline soils tend to be deficient in humus and less able to hold moisture. This problem may be compounded by the tendency in arid or semiarid regions for lime to collect in the subsoil, forming an impenetrable

▼ **Geranium family** Wild and cultivated geraniums — pink *Geranium endressii* and violet-blue *G.* x *magnificum* — thrive in dry alkaline soil. The large-leaved pink *Polygonum bistorta* and purple *Iris sibirica* are good companions.

hardpan known as caliche. This layer impedes the growth of plant roots and prevents rain or irrigation water from wetting the soil to any depth.

Soil improvement
The best solution to caliche is to break up this layer either by mechanical or manual means. An alternative approach to reducing the threat of drought lies in boosting the soil's organic content. Dig in substantial quantities of some organic material such as compost or well-rotted manure at planting time — increasing the organic content by 10 percent or more. Thereafter, maintain an organic mulch such as shredded bark around the base of plantings. Boosting the soil's organic

◄ **New York asters** Fall-flowering *Aster novi-belgii* thrives in alkaline soil, provided it is fertile and moisture retentive but not waterlogged. A sunny site is essential.

▼ **Pasqueflowers** The beautiful pasqueflower *(Pulsatilla vulgaris)* grows wild on limy grasslands. In the garden it flourishes in alkaline soil and appreciates a mulch of limestone chips to keep its roots cool and its crown dry.

content will not only increase its ability to hold water, it will also enhance its fertility. Finally, because most rotting organic matter is acid, adding it helps to reduce the soil's alkalinity.

Peat, especially sphagnum peat, is highly acidic, and those who garden in excessively alkaline soils or those who wish to grow acid-loving plants in alkaline-soil regions may be advised to dig peat into their gardens to "correct" the pH. This is an expensive remedy, however, if the garden is large.

Rather than digging the whole bed, it is much easier to create favorable soil conditions around the roots of each individual plant. Such preparation is beneficial for permanent plants, such as trees and shrubs. When planting, incorporate a generous layer of organic matter with the soil in the bottom of the planting hole and with the soil used to fill in around the sides of the plant's root ball.

Ground-cover plants may be used as a living mulch. Once the stems knit and the foliage covers the bed, the ground cover will act

▲ **Alkaline-tolerant brooms** Spring- and summer-flowering brooms *(Genista)* grow well in either acid or neutral soil, and they actually bloom best on soil that is poor and well drained.

▼ **Red valerian** In the wild, red valerian *(Centranthus ruber)* decorates the thin soil on cliff faces, rocks, and limestone quarries with its fiery red flowers. It seeds itself in the tiniest wall cracks.

▲ **Fertile columbines** Columbines (*Aquilegia*) like rich and moisture-retentive alkaline soils. If allowed to set seed, they interbreed to produce mixed colors.

▼ **Lime-loving clematis** The large-flowered clematis hybrids are exuberant in alkaline soil. Make sure that the soil doesn't dry out.

as a conventional mulch does by reducing evaporation from the soil and by keeping the soil cool.

Choosing plants

You will get better results and save yourself a lot of work by selecting suitable plants. Few plants insist on lime, but many are as happy in it as they are in neutral or acid soil.

If your soil is rich in lime, take your cue from the local flora. Native trees and shrubs found in free-draining alkaline soil include the catalpas (*Catalpa bignonioides* and *C. speciosa*), pecan, beautyberry (*Callicarpa americana*), acacias, box elder (*Acer negundo*), red osier (*Cornus sericea*), honey and black locusts (*Gleditsia triacanthos* and *Robinia pseudoacacia*), juniper, American elderberry, and sassafrass tree (*Sassafrass albidum*). All are worth growing.

Of introduced garden plants, buddleia, deutzia, forsythia, fuchsia, laburnum, lilac, and philadelphus are ideal shrubs for alkaline soil. Most climbing roses tolerate alkaline soil, and hybrid clematises love it. Aubrieta, *Aurinia saxatilis*, and other Cruciferae

family members thrive in alkaline soil, as do peonies, gypsophilas, red-hot pokers, and daylilies.

As a rule, gray-leaved plants enjoy the perfect drainage of alkaline soils, if there is ample sun. Most bulbs native to hot, dry climates are also at home in sunny alkaline sites. These include colchicums, cyclamens, and lilies.

However, not all plants that tolerate alkalinity can also tolerate dry, gritty soil. Most hybrid bush roses, for example, prefer the less alkaline and richer, more moisture-retentive heavy clay.

▶ **Ornamental onions** These summer-flowering *Allium* bulbs grow quite happily in alkaline soils, as do their relatives — leeks, onions, and chives. Good drainage is essential, as is an open and sunny site.

PLANTS FOR ALKALINE SOIL

	NAME	DESCRIPTION	HEIGHT	SPREAD	SITE
SHRUBS AND TREES	*Buddleia* species (buddleia)	Deciduous; spikes of purple, mauve, or white flowers, or orange globes in summer	5-15 ft (1.5-4.5 m)	5-12 ft (1.5-3.6 m)	Any soil; full sun
	Buxus sempervirens (boxwood)	Evergreen with glossy small leaves; variegated and dwarf forms	10 ft (3 m)	4-6 ft (1.2-1.8 m)	Well-drained soil; full sun or light shade
	Ceanothus species (California lilac)	Deciduous or evergreen; fluffy blue flowers in late spring and summer	7-20 ft (2.1-6 m)	7-20 ft (2.1-6 m)	Light soil; mainly alkaline tolerant; full sun; shelter
	Ceratostigma willmottianum (Chinese plumbago)	Deciduous; blue flowers in late summer; good fall foliage color	3 ft (90 cm)	3 ft (90 cm)	Well-drained soil; sun; shelter
	Clematis species and hybrids (clematis)	Climbers, usually deciduous; pink, red, white, or mauve flowers from spring to fall	7-25 ft (2.1-7.5 m)	7-25 ft (2.1-7.5 m)	Well-drained soil; sun but roots shaded
	Deutzia species (deutzia)	Deciduous; masses of starry white or pink flowers in early summer	4-6 ft (1.2-1.8 m)	4-6 ft (1.2-1.8 m)	Tolerant of most conditions
	Euonymus species (euonymus)	Evergreen or deciduous; some species have attractive berries	1-15 ft (30-450 cm)	6-15 ft (1.8-4.5 m)	Any well-drained soil; sun or shade
	Forsythia species (forsythia)	Deciduous; bell-shaped yellow flowers along leafless branches in spring	5-10 ft (1.5-3 m)	5-10 ft (1.5-3 m)	Well-drained soil; sun or shade
	Genista species (broom)	Deciduous; tiny yellow pealike flowers in spring or summer	1-10 ft (30-300 cm)	1-10 ft (30-300 cm)	Well-drained, light to poor soil; alkaline tolerant; sun
	Hedera species (ivy)	Evergreen, self-clinging climbers; many variegated forms available	15-50 ft (4.5-15 m)	15-50 ft (4.5-15 m)	Tolerant of most conditions
	Juniperus species (juniper)	Evergreen conifers; dwarf and colored foliage forms available	1½-18 ft (45-540 cm)	1½-10 ft (45-300 cm)	Well-drained soil; sun
	Philadelphus species (mock orange)	Deciduous; white, heavily scented, cup-shaped flowers in late spring and early summer	4-10 ft (1.2-3 m)	4-10 ft (1.2-3 m)	Well-drained soil; sun or light shade
	Santolina species (lavender cotton)	Ever-gray; delicate silvery foliage and yellow buttonlike flowers in summer	2-2½ ft (60-75 cm)	3-4 ft (90-120 cm)	Well-drained, light soil; sun
	Spiraea species (spirea)	Deciduous; clusters of white, pink, or rosy flowers in summer	2-9 ft (60-270 cm)	3-10 ft (90-300 cm)	Any soil; full sun
	Taxus species (yew)	Evergreen conifers; dwarf and golden forms available; red or yellow berries	2½-20 ft (75-600 cm)	2½-20 ft (75-600 cm)	Well-drained soil; sun or light shade

PLANTS FOR ALKALINE SOIL					
	NAME	DESCRIPTION	HEIGHT	SPREAD	SITE
HERBACEOUS PERENNIALS	*Acanthus* species (bear's breeches)	Spikes of mauve-gray flowers in summer; attractive, sometimes spiny leaves	4 ft (1.2 m)	3 ft (90 cm)	Well-drained soil; sun or semishade
	Agapanthus species (African lily)	Rounded heads of blue or white flowers in late summer	2-3 ft (60-90 cm)	1½-2 ft (45-60 cm)	Deep, rich, well-drained soil; sun
	Alchemilla mollis (lady's mantle)	Masses of tiny yellow-green flowers in summer; handsome gray-green leaves	1-1½ ft (30-45 cm)	1½ ft (45 cm)	Tolerant of most conditions
	Anchusa species (alkanet, bugloss)	Rich blue saucer-shaped flowers in early summer or midsummer	2-60 in (5-150 cm)	3-18 in (7.5-45 cm)	Well-drained soil; full sun
	Anemone species (anemone)	Cup-shaped flowers in spring or fall; finely cut leaves	6-48 in (15-120 cm)	4-24 in (10-60 cm)	Moist, rich, well-drained soil; light shade or sun
	Aquilegia species (columbine)	Spurred flowers in white, pink, blue, or purple in early summer	6-36 in (15-90 cm)	6-24 in (15-60 cm)	Moist, rich, well-drained soil; sun or light shade
	Aster species (New York aster)	Daisylike flowers in white, pink, mauve, or purple in late summer	1½-4 ft (45-120 cm)	1-2 ft (30-60 cm)	Moist, rich, well-drained soil; sun
	Aubrieta deltoidea (aubrieta, rock cress)	Profuse tiny pink, mauve, purple, or white flowers from late spring to early summer	6-8 in (15-20 cm)	1-2 ft (30-60 cm)	Well-drained, even poor soil; full sun
	Aurinia saxatilis (basket-of-gold)	Sprays of brilliant golden yellow flowers above silver-gray leaves in late spring	6-12 in (15-30 cm)	1½-2ft (45-60 cm)	Well-drained, even poor soil; full sun
	Bergenia species (bergenia)	Evergreen; spikes of pink flowers in late winter or early spring	1-2 ft (30-60 cm)	1½-2 ft (45-60 cm)	Tolerant of most conditions; shade
	Centranthus ruber (red valerian)	Deep pink, red, or white flowers all summer long	2-3 ft (60-90 cm)	1-2 ft (30-60 cm)	Well-drained, even poor soil; sun
	Dianthus species (carnations, pinks)	Variously colored flowers; grayish grassy leaves	2-36 in (5-90 cm)	6-18 in (15-45 cm)	Well-drained, light soil; sun
	Echinops ritro (globe thistle)	Globes of steely blue flowers in summer; dark green thistlelike leaves	4 ft (1.2 m)	2 ft (60 cm)	Any well-drained soil; sun
	Erigeron species (fleabane)	Daisylike flowers in rose, pink, mauve, or red in summer	4-24 in (10-60 cm)	2 ft (60 cm)	Moist, well-drained soil; sun
	Geranium species (cranesbill)	Flat, saucer-shaped flowers in various colors in summer; attractive leaves	6-30 in (15-75 cm)	1-2½ ft (30-75 cm)	Well-drained soil; sun or shade
	Helichrysum species (helichrysum)	Aromatic silver leaves and yellow flowers in summer	3-6 ft (90-180 cm)	4-6 ft (1.2-1.8 m)	Well-drained, light soil; sun
	Hemerocallis species (daylily)	Yellow, orange, pink, or red trumpet-shaped flowers in summer	1-3½ ft (30-105 cm)	8-36 in (20-90 cm)	Tolerant of most conditions except deep shade
	Kniphofia species (red-hot poker)	Spikes of tubular red, yellow, orange, or cream flowers in summer	2½-3 ft (75-90 cm)	2-4 ft (60-120 cm)	Well-drained, even poor soil; sun
	Linum species (flax)	Saucer-shaped blue, yellow, or scarlet flowers in summer	6-24 in (15-60 cm)	8-12 in (20-30 cm)	Well-drained soil; sun
	Paeonia species (peony)	Large, single or double red, pink, or white flowers in spring or summer	2-4 ft (60-120 cm)	2-3 ft (60-90 cm)	Well-drained, fertile soil; sun or light shade
	Phlox species (phlox)	Clusters of pink, white, mauve, or rose flowers in late summer	4-36 in (10-90 cm)	1½-3 ft (45-90 cm)	Well-drained, moist soil; sun or light shade
	Polemonium species (Jacob's ladder)	Blue, pink, or white cup-shaped flowers in late spring or summer	1-2½ ft (30-75 cm)	1-1½ ft (30-45 cm)	Well-drained, moist soil; sun or shade
	Polygonum bistorta (snakeweed)	Spikes of pink-red flowers in early summer; large light green leaves	3 ft (90 cm)	2 ft (60 cm)	Well-drained soil; sun or light shade
	Stachys byzantina (lamb's ears)	Soft, furry gray leaves; some forms carry spikes of small pink flowers in summer	1-1½ ft (30-45 cm)	1 ft (30 cm)	Well-drained soil; full sun
BULBS	*Allium* species (ornamental onions)	Rounded heads of white, yellow, red, or purple flowers in spring or summer	6-48 in (15-120 cm)	6-12 in (15-30 cm)	Well-drained, even poor soil; sun
	Crocosmia x *crocosmiiflora* (montebretia)	Orange, yellow, or red flowers from midsummer to late fall	2-2½ ft (60-75 cm)	6 in (15 cm)	Open, well-drained soil; full sun
	Gladiolus species and hybrids (sword lily)	Spikes of trumpet-shaped flowers from midsummer to midfall	1-5 ft (30-150 cm)	6 in (15 cm)	Humus-rich, well-drained soil; sun
	Iris species (iris)	Flowers in various colors and seasons, depending on species	8-48 in (20-120 cm)	8-16 in (20-40 cm)	Well-drained, not too limy soil; sun

INDEX

ACKNOWLEDGMENTS

Photographers' credits
Agence Bamboo/Arnaud Descat 162-163 (t); Gillian Beckett 83 (b); Biofotos/Heather Angel 132 (b); Brian Carter 166 (br); Eric Crichton 6, 9, 17 (b), 19, 32 (t), 34 (t), 37, 84 (t), 98 (b), 102, 125-131, 138 (tr), 167, 168 (b), 169 (b), 170-171; Eric Crichton/Hazel Dipple 87-88, 90-92; Eric Crichton/G. Tonge 25-30; Eric Crichton/Mrs. Vlasto 53-58; Geoff Dann 32 (b); Geoff Dann/Mr. and Mrs. Jonzen 59-62; Eaglemoss (Eric Crichton) 113-118, (Andrew Lawson/M. Blumson) 115-156, 158-160; Phillipe Ferret 94(tl), 96, 137(b), 164(b); John Glover 103(b), 104, 106, 135(t), 137(t); Derek & Lyn Gould 21, 23-24; Garden Picture Library (Brian Carter) 162-163(b), 169(t),

(Marijke Heuff) 14(b), (Perdereau/Thomas) 162 (bl), (Stephen Robson) 8; Jerry Harpur/Ken Akers 40; Jerry Harpur/Mackenzie Bell 149-151, 153-154; Marijke Heuff Amsterdam 93; Neil Holmes 139(t); Insight Picture Library (Linda Burgess) 94(tr), 132(t); IPC Magazines/Robert Harding Syndication 14(t); Patrick Johns 11(b); Lamontagne 95, 136; Georges Leveque 63, 65-68, 82, 85; George Leveque/Tymen Lannurien 47-52; S&O Mathews 39, 135(b); Tania Midgely 1, 16-17, 35(t), 103(t), 161; Natural Image (Robin Fletcher) 97, (Bob Gibbons) 101, 164(t); John Neubauer 107-112, 119-124; Clive Nichols 4-5, 100, Back Cover; Suzanne O'Connell 142-148; Phillipe Perdereau 38(t), 41-46, 166(bl); Photos Horticultural 10, 13, 15, 18, 20, 33, 34-35, 38(b), 81, 83(t), 84(b), 98(t), 138(tl,b), 139(b),

166(t), 168(t); Trevor Richards 71-76; Harry Smith Collection 11(t), 12, 31, 165; Elizabeth Whiting Associates (Karl-Dietrich Buhler) 99, (Rodney Hyatt) Front cover, (Andrew Lawson/Simon Driver) 77-78, 80, (Marie O'Hara) 2-3, (Peter Wolosynski) 70; Linda Yang 36.

Illustrators
Lyn Chadwick 157, 22-23, 44-45, 79; Colin Emberson 136; Josephine Martin 137; Vivien Monument 48-49, 88-89; Reader's Digest 102, 104, 161-164, (Barbara Walker) 40, (Dick Bonson) 96, (Gill Tomblin) 39, (Sarah Fox-Davies) 95; Cheryl Willbrahn 64-65; Claire Wright 99.

Index compiled by Sidney Wolfe Cohen.